Sane

Mental Illness, Addiction, and the Twelve Steps

Marya Hornbacher

Hazelden
Publishing

Hazelden Publishing
Center City, Minnesota
hazelden.org/bookstore

Library of Congress Cataloging-in-Publication Data
Hornbacher, Marya, 1974-
    Sane : mental illness, addiction, and the twelve steps / by Marya Hornbacher.
        p. cm.
    ISBN 978-1-59285-824-8
    1. Alcoholism--Treatment. 2. Mental illness. 3. Alcoholics Anonymous. 4. Twelve-step programs   I. Title.
    HV5278.H67 2010
    616.86'06--dc22

                                                              2010006789

Editor's note
The names, details, and circumstances have been changed to protect the privacy of those mentioned in this publication.
This publication is not intended as a substitute for the advice of health care professionals.
Alcoholics Anonymous and AA are registered trademarks of Alcoholics Anonymous World Services, Inc.

Cover design by Theresa Jaeger Gedig
Interior design by David Spohn
Typesetting by BookMobile Design and Publishing Services

Contents

Foreword

There are many poignant yet practical sayings in Twelve Step recovery. When it comes to choosing a sponsor, it is often advised to select a person who *knows* the way, *goes* the way, and can *show* the way. Each of these three ingredients would seem rather important in identifying a person to help with the daunting task of recovery from a co-occurring mental health and substance use problem.

Marya Hornbacher *knows* the way, *goes* the way, and *shows* the way. *Sane* is an excellent bridge to the remarkable and miraculous transformation that can take place through the fellowship and wisdom of the Twelve Step program of recovery. What Marya Hornbacher does in *Sane* is interpret these twelve suggested Steps for people with co-occurring disorders, making them understandable, while anticipating and addressing common concerns and questions. She translates recovery terminology that on the surface may seem at odds with having a mental health problem, and makes it accessible to anyone.

The evidence is in: peer recovery groups such as Alcoholics Anonymous and Narcotics Anonymous really work. Yet research shows that people with mental disorders—particularly severe ones such as bipolar disorder, schizophrenia, PTSD, or severe depression or anxiety—don't connect with AA or NA as successfully as people with more moderate emotional problems do. And even when they do connect, they're not as successful in sustaining recovery over time.

There are probably many reasons for this. Some have to do with the nature of these mental health problems, which can be characterized by symptoms of avoidance, isolation, withdrawal, and negativity that can preempt action. Moreover, not all Twelve Step recovery groups are open to people with severe mental health issues. This is remarkable, if not paradoxical, given that groups such as AA were originally formed to offer social support and solutions to individuals who often felt ashamed and socially marginalized by their disease. The goal was to create a group that was inclusive and accepting, not exclusive and judgmental. Fortunately, most peer recovery support meetings retain the ambiance of acceptance and tolerance. The primary purpose remains, in essence, to try to get sober and help others in doing so.

Still, for the person with co-occurring disorders, the thought of going to a recovery support group meeting can be terrifying. In fact, the idea provokes anxiety for just about anyone, but in this case the prospect is so threatening that it is often avoided at all costs. So, since most alcoholics and addicts also have a mental health problem, how do any of them ever make it to a meeting, let alone stick around long enough to get clean and sober and engage in sustained recovery? We don't know. It may be a matter of miracles, willingness, desperation, social support, serendipity, timing, good luck, or simply the exhaustion of all other options.

In this book, Marya Hornbacher finds the way through or around these perceived barriers, debunking common mythologies about Twelve Step meetings. Reading *Sane* is akin to having an AA or NA sponsor. This book serves as the introduction, the guide, and the validation of personal experience. *Sane* offers ways of managing the complexity, of making it all seem okay.

Mark P. McGovern, Ph.D.
Department of Psychiatry
Dartmouth Medical School

Preface

I REMEMBER THE FIRST TIME I READ the Twelve Steps at an Alcoholics Anonymous meeting. I sat down with my cup of coffee, avoiding everyone's eyes, and stared at the Steps on a poster on the wall. I made it through Step One all right—didn't make a lot of sense to me, but I got the general idea—and then I came to Step Two: *Came to believe that a Power greater than ourselves could restore us to sanity.*

I tripped over the word *sanity*, nearly laughed out loud, and then nearly cried.

"Sanity" was not something I was particularly familiar with. I have a mental illness, bipolar disorder, and that in itself had taken from me time and again the sanity I desperately wanted. Compounded by years of the insanity of alcoholism and addiction, I was, at that time, pretty well convinced that sanity was something I could never hope for. I sat there as that AA meeting was called to order, slumped in my chair, and wondered if I should just walk out. I thought there was no way I could ever have what the people around me seemed to have: laughter, companionship, stability—and sanity.

I was very wrong. The Twelve Steps have led me on a fascinating, often difficult, but eventually rewarding and powerful journey to a place of ever-increasing sanity and stability.

In this book I try to stay true to Twelve Step recovery basics while setting out some suggestions and ideas for how they can be practiced by someone who deals with mental illness. In many ways, we will work the Steps no differently than anyone else—addiction is addiction. But the fact is, there are certain challenges the Steps appear to pose on first glance that may make them seem intimidating, or even impossible, for those of us with mental illness. They are by no means impossible, and they don't have to be intimidating. My goal is to honestly address the real challenges that people with a mental illness face as they apply the Steps in their Twelve Step support group and in all areas of their recovery.

Of course the Steps aren't the only support that we need to maintain mental wellness. They didn't cure my mental illness, and they won't. That's not their function, and in fact, we shouldn't expect them to be a miracle cure for anything. But practiced thoroughly, consistently, and in the sequence they were written, they can light the way on what is sometimes a very confusing path to recovery from addiction and to successful management of a mental health disorder. The Twelve Steps, in conjunction with all the other essential supports to mental health, are exactly what AA's Big Book says they can be: they are "a program for living."

When I was still caught in active addiction and therefore unable to manage my mental illness, basic *living* was a constant struggle. That's why my work in a Twelve Step program was so vital: I needed, first and foremost, to maintain my sobriety, because without sobriety, I have no hope of managing my mental illness. Mental illness is a genetic brain disorder, and the brain chemistry of people who have it cannot tolerate further disturbance by addiction to chemicals or compulsive behavior. Like many of you reading this, I had to learn that the hard way. The insanity of addiction—and addiction is itself a mental disorder—fuels other mental disorders like gasoline feeds a raging fire. Active addiction simply isn't an option for us, and we must do everything necessary to find release from our obsession with addictive substances and behaviors. Working the Steps is the best way I, and millions like me, have found to do that.

By awakening qualities such as acceptance, willingness, humility, and honesty, the Twelve Steps offer a design for living that allows me not only to better manage my mental illness but to regain my sense of values. Mental wellness and sobriety have everything to do with making good choices and taking right action. As we learn to do this by working the Steps and seeking others' help in our peer support group meetings, we truly do come to a place of sanity.

This book also tries to bridge the gap some of us have felt between our understanding of mental illness and the inaccurate perceptions of it that we may have encountered in Twelve Step groups. Not everyone in recovery has a firm grasp of what mental illness is or how it needs to be treated. We may have run into people who were unaware that mental illnesses are physical diseases of the brain, or people who didn't understand that psychiatric medication is often an essential part of our treatment. People who don't know these things may have told us that our medication was the same as "using," or told us that our mental health concerns should be kept out of our Twelve Step meetings. This message can be alienating and can turn a person off from Twelve Step programs. In this book, I hope that readers will find that they are not alone with these experiences, that there are millions of us dealing with both mental illness and addiction who have found remarkable recovery in these programs despite the challenges.

Above all, this book is nothing more than one person's take on the Steps. In recovery, all we really have to offer is our own perspective and our own "experience, strength, and hope." If by reading this book, people in similar circumstances feel like they have company as they walk the road to recovery, then it will have been a success. I have had good company on my walk, and I count myself incredibly lucky for that. I hope that you will write in this book, underline, scribble out, argue, agree, dispute—in short, that you will find it a useful companion in an ongoing dialogue as you make your way out of the chaos of addiction and mental illness and into the light of day.

Acknowledgments

MANY THANKS TO MY SUPERB EDITOR at Hazelden, Sid Farrar. Much gratitude also to the members of my home group, my wonderful sponsor, and all my sponsees—it's you who truly keep me sober and sane.

Acceptance

We admitted we were powerless over alcohol—
that our lives had become unmanageable.

I DON'T KNOW WHICH WAS THE STRANGER, more terrifying moment: the moment when a psychiatrist told me I had a mental illness, or the moment I realized I was an alcoholic, through and through. I remember both moments clearly: my stomach dropped, the room seemed cold, and I wanted to run for the door. When it came time for me to face facts, I didn't do it. Not that first time. The fear that accompanied those simple facts—that I have a mental illness, that I am an alcoholic—was so overwhelming that I did what fear told me to do: I hid.

Addicts are good at hiding—for a while. We've turned it into an art form. We hide from our families, our friends, our employers; some of us feel we are hiding from God. We are capable of believing the ridiculous notion that no one can see what's really going on. No one really knows how sad and sick and dependent we are. People with mental illness often share this skill at hiding. The world we live in tells us that mental illness is something to be ashamed of, and heaven knows we feel that shame—and we do all we can to hide our illness from that judging world, from our fellows, and often from ourselves.

So by the time we addicts or alcoholics with mental illness have reached a place of complete defeat—by the time we realize that *our lives have become unmanageable*—we are living under so many layers of shame, deception, denial, and fear that it seems at first impossible to dig ourselves out. We are used to the dark, lonely place where we've lived for so long. We're used to the company of our substance of choice, the comfort of our habitual terror, the pain of our mental illness. These things are more familiar than what the Twelve Steps promise: a life in a community of people who have found a better way to live. To the practicing addict with mental illness, a life up there in the light seems almost as frightening as a life down here in her own private hell.

But we must reach for that life if we want to survive.

Addicts, mentally ill or not, must all come to a turning point where they recognize that there is no future ahead on the road they're walking, and realize that it's time for them to turn down a new road. That moment of realization is rarely a calm one. It often takes hitting the wall pretty hard—often more than once—before we see the futility of trying to live the way we were. From the *Twelve Steps and Twelve Traditions:* "We perceive that only through utter defeat are we able to take our first steps toward liberation and strength."

And that is where we're headed when we set out with Step One: toward liberation and strength.

When I first came into the program, I found the idea of admitting defeat insane. I already *felt* defeated, by my illness, by my addiction, by my entire life. Why were these people asking me to go one step further and admit *complete* defeat—admit, in short, that I was wholly and completely powerless? I insisted that I would get sober anyway, whether I admitted powerlessness or not. Couldn't I just hang on to *some* sense of control over my life? The answer my sponsor gave me was a resounding *no.*

When I was first faced with the need to admit powerlessness, I told my sponsor she didn't understand mental illness—if she understood the horrible feeling of being literally out of control of one's own mind, she would never try to make me feel even less power than I already did. I believed, at first, that Step One would be impossible for me. I believed my mental illness would make it too painful. I believed it would be too excruciating, too terrifying, to admit total powerlessness over my addiction and over my life when I already felt so terribly helpless.

But I have come to see this differently. I have come to see the First Step as one that my mental illness allows me to understand with particular clarity. I began to apply what I know about mental illness to what I was learning about addiction, and I began to listen to what I was being told about how addiction could be overcome.

Who knows better than we do a true sense of helplessness over the body and mind? Our mental illnesses do not define us, but they are part of the very bodies we live in and part of the very makeup of our minds. My mental illness is inscribed on my genes and expressed in my very thoughts—it's that close to me. Working the Twelve Steps, I began to learn that addiction is an illness of body and mind as well. It is defined as a mental illness in the *Diagnostic and Statistical Manual of Mental Disorders*, a compendium of psychiatric diagnoses that lists and defines them. It is an allergy of the body that manifests itself as an obsession of the mind. It is passed through families in the genes, just as other mental illnesses are. People who suffer from addiction are physically different from people who do not; our bodies respond to certain substances and behaviors differently than do healthy, non-addicted bodies.

The brain is a complicated organ, and we are only just beginning to understand it. But one thing is clear: many people who deal with typical mental illness also deal with the mental illness of addiction. And while that dual diagnosis can at times seem like a bum deal, it also offers those of us who have typical mental illness *and* addiction some wonderful opportunities.

The Twelve Steps, it is often said, are a program for living. Each Step is important in its own right, but as we work them one by one, we begin to see how they work together to literally change us and offer us a new way of life. They are not just a way of keeping the plug in the jug. And the First Step—admitting we are powerless and that our lives are out of control—is how we begin to work that larger program, how we begin to create that change in ourselves, and how we embark on that new way of living.

It's important to remember that the First Step isn't taken for its own sake—we aren't admitting powerlessness as an end in itself. The First Step is not there just to make us feel terrified and out of control. It's there to get us started on our way through the rest of the Steps, to get us started on this journey to a new life. It's there to help us let go of our vise grip on the delusions that keep us sick. Picture Step One as the moment when you open your hands and let all the deceptions, denial, shame, and fear drop to the ground. Then walk away.

The same things that keep us trapped in active addictions prevent us from dealing in a healthy way with our mental illness. We tell ourselves: It isn't that bad. No one can tell. It isn't hurting anyone but me. Everyone's making a big deal out of nothing. Or we tell ourselves: It's hopeless. No one can help me. There's no point in trying. I'm going to die this way. There's no way out. Or we tell ourselves: If I just ignore it, it will go away. If I just pretend this isn't happening, maybe it will stop.

These are delusions, and they are fatal. Until we honestly face our mental illness and do all we can to treat and manage it, we will continue to be limited and harmed by it; until we honestly face our addiction and do all we can to recover from it, we will continue to live in this hell of isolation, smashed dreams, hopelessness, and despair. We cannot choose one or the other: we cannot say, I will deal with my mental illness but continue in my addiction; and we cannot say, I will sober up but ignore my mental illness. To try to choose is foolish. The simple fact is that continuing to use drugs and alcohol makes our mental illness worse and prevents our medication from having the necessary effects. We can't hope for any improvement in our mental illness while we are still using. Both our mental illness and our addiction must be dealt with—dealt with head-on and at once.

The first time I went to a Twelve Step meeting, I was badly hung over and several days off the medications I needed. I remember sitting in the meeting room, staring at the signs with the Twelve Steps that hung on the wall. It was blindingly sunny, I felt like the floor was swimming, and I was peering at the words. I could not make head or tail of what they said. I mean, I could read them, but I just couldn't make sense of what they meant. I read through them several times and finally gave up and just focused on the First Step.

Admitted we were powerless over alcohol—well, I wasn't so sure about that. Sure, I drank a lot. Too much. I knew that. But *powerless?* It seemed like an awfully strong word.

. . . and that our lives had become unmanageable. Now, *that* I could get behind. No question my life was unmanageable. My life was a raging mess. Everyone I knew had a theory about why it was such a mess—I drank too much, I needed more therapy, I worked too hard, I didn't sleep enough, I kept going off my meds. And I had a theory, too: I was just a screwup, had always been a screwup, and would always be a screwup, no matter what I did.

So, sitting in that meeting room, I couldn't quite explain why I was hit with the realization that those Steps on the wall were a lifeboat, and I was sinking, and I needed to hang on for dear life.

You know what? I didn't. I walked out of the meeting and went home and took my meds with a beer. I did what I always did—I hid.

My life wasn't really unmanageable, I decided. And I *certainly* wasn't powerless over alcohol.

Fast-forward just a few months: I'm sitting in a snowbank on the sidewalk of a wide, dirty, empty street. It's maybe seven o'clock in the morning. The sun's just coming up, and I'm out of booze. I'm peering into the mouth of the bottle, as if I'll find some more in there if I look real hard. I'm trying to stand up but am too drunk to get out of the snowbank. Freezing cold, wet, and filthy, I realize the liquor store won't open for another three hours. I start to cry.

I am powerless over alcohol. And my life has become seriously unmanageable.

Complete defeat.

In other words: a new beginning.

Every addict wants the magic bullet, the moment of revelation where we say, "Aha!" and it all becomes clear. Sadly, few of us have such a moment. My snowbank realization that I was pretty well done for if I didn't get some help was followed by months and months of fighting. Fighting other people, fighting the program, fighting myself. Fighting, first and foremost, the First Step. Fighting the idea that I was powerless, that alcohol and mental illness were bigger than I was, that I needed to take action to recover if I wanted to survive.

Waiting around for salvation just wasn't going to cut it anymore. Waiting for it to all go away overnight wasn't one of my options. I had to act, and fast.

But the simple fact that I *could* act—that there *was* something that could be done if I chose to do it, there *was* a way out of the hell in which I was living—was a revelation. For so long, I had believed that there was no hope for me. No hope for a mentally ill alcoholic who couldn't seem to get either her mental illness or her alcoholism under control. I was a crazy drunk, and there was nothing I could do, nothing that could be done for me. Helpless and hopeless, I had given up all faith in the world and had lost all faith in myself.

The Twelve Steps are a path up and out of that isolated, hopeless, helpless place. They are a series of actions I can take, and I take them in the company of others. Sobriety is not something that can be found alone; we need the help and company of our fellows. This maxim is simple but crucial: don't drink, read the Big Book, and go to meetings. Meetings are enormously important to the maintenance of sobriety and the development of a sober life. There, we find our way out of isolation by listening to the stories of other sober people who are making a new life for themselves. After years of disaffection and alienation from the world, we find at meetings a true community of people with whom we connect. The people we find at meetings are working the Steps alongside us and have much wisdom and experience to share. They help us see the Steps for what they are: hope when I am hopeless, and help when I think there is no help for me. The Big Book says that these Steps can work "no matter how far down the scale we have gone." Millions of recovering people can testify to the truth of that statement. And so, beginning wherever we are, knowing we are not alone, we take that First Step: we admit that we are powerless, and that admission sets us free.

The admission of powerlessness lifts the burden of delusion we carry, the delusion that if we just try hard enough, we can master the substance that has us in its grip. Every addict has labored under this delusion—that we can, by force of will, gain control over the substance to which we're addicted, and that our failure to do that is simply more proof that we are failures as people. We who have a mental illness are already acquainted with this feeling of failure. How many times have we tried to control our mental illness—a physical disease—by "pulling ourselves up by our bootstraps," by "positive thinking," by trying to simply *will* our illness away? And how well has that worked? Neither mental illness nor addiction can be willed away; they both require serious action proportionate to the seriousness of the disease.

We must recognize that, as addicts, our bodies were constructed with a perverse will to self-destruct: we are chemically inclined to consume a substance that will ultimately consume us. The fact that we have a mental illness makes us doubly vulnerable to addiction. The Big Book has it right: "The delusion we are like other people, or presently may be, has to be smashed." When we admit that we are powerless—over the fact that we have a mental illness and over the substance to which we have become addicted—we are prepared to take action that will put us back in charge of our lives.

For a long time, I grappled with the second part of the First Step: "our lives had become unmanageable." I could concede that it was true—my life was clearly out of control. But that had always been the case. Was it because I was an addict, or because I had a mental illness? Before I got sober, I, like a lot of us, was pretty sure I drank to "self-medicate." (There's a big difference between unhealthy "self-medication" and taking the medications that we truly need. The medications that target our imbalanced chemistry return us to a stable state where we are at our healthiest and most functional;

street drugs and alcohol, the things we use to "self-medicate," further imbalance our chemistry, make us yet more unstable, and take away our ability to function.) I told myself I drank to deal with the pain of mental illness, and that if I wasn't mentally ill, I wouldn't have so much to drink about. This was one of many ways in which the old self-pity showed its face—the truth of the matter is that plenty of people deal with their mental illness without getting smashed every night. Well, then (I said), maybe I'm really just an alcoholic and not mentally ill at all. Maybe if I sober up, the mental illness will go away. Wishful thinking. The fact is that I am mentally ill *and* alcoholic. My life was unmanageable because I wasn't dealing with *either.*

And that's an important point: it wasn't that mental illness was *making* my life unmanageable, or that alcohol was. It was that I wasn't *dealing* with these things. Because life with a mental illness *can* be manageable, and millions of sober addicts will be glad to tell you that life after addiction is manageable as well. The key word, again, is action.

It may seem strange to speak of acceptance as action, but that's the action required to take Step One. The Step requires radical acceptance. Acceptance of powerlessness, acceptance that our lives are truly and completely unmanageable, acceptance that we have reached a stage of complete defeat. Only when we accept these truths will we reach the willingness required to take the next eleven Steps. Step One does not tell us we are failures; it shows us that the way we have been doing things has failed. Seeing clearly, we can assess the reality of our lives and situations and accept that we need to live a new way. This new way of living exists and can be obtained by working the Steps.

It may be that the First Step is particularly uncomfortable for someone with mental illness. I know that it was the hardest Step for me to take. I wanted so badly to cling to the notion that I really was all right, that I really would get things under control if I just tried a little harder, that I *wasn't* powerless. The words "complete defeat" made me feel sick. That was what I was so scared of—the idea that I had been defeated, by mental illness, by alcohol—and what I fought so hard against. I was willing to live in total denial as long as I could cling to the delusion that I wasn't beaten yet. But that denial was killing me. That unwillingness to face facts, to accept reality, was a deadly form of fear and had to be overcome. We are not being asked to *stay* in a place of complete defeat. We are being offered a way out.

Working a program will not cure my mental illness, but in working a program, I learn things that can help me manage it. I learn the power of surrender. I surrender to the truth, facing the reality of my mental illness and my addiction, and that surrender sets me free. I am now free to take action on my own behalf: I now choose to manage my mental illness, and I now choose to live a sober life. Step One is where that surrender takes place.

Step One divests us of the last of our delusions. It cleans the slate. It clears the fog before our eyes and shows us a future we had not thought possible for ourselves. Having admitted powerlessness, we are now possessed of the liberation and strength we need to take Step Two.

Sanity

*Came to believe that a Power greater
than ourselves could restore us to sanity.*

IN STEP ONE, OUR DELUSIONS WERE SMASHED. We saw clearly that we could not go on living the way we were, and that something had to change; we saw the insanity of our lives and recognized that it had to stop. In Step Two, we take action based on that knowledge. We go in search of sanity and hope.

For some of us, Step Two may pose some challenges. First, there is the challenge of believing in a Power greater than ourselves; then there is the challenge of actually believing that sanity *can* be restored. Many addicts with mental illness reach Step Two and stumble.

Many of us balk outright at the very suggestion that we'll need anything like God to get sober, and many despair at the idea that sanity can ever be ours. But it is possible for each of us to find a way to understand and work this Step, and to reap its enormous rewards. Step Two is a critical moment in our journey toward sobriety and the sanity it brings. It isn't the insurmountable hurdle it seems on first examination. All this Step requires is an open mind.

I remember my very first shot at getting sober. I'd been on and off my medication for some time and was drinking day in, day out. I knew I had to stop, but I just couldn't make it happen on my own. In desperation, I called Alcoholics Anonymous and was directed to the closest meeting. I sat shaking in my folding chair while all around me people were inexplicably jolly and laughing. The meeting began, but I was hardly aware of it—it had been a long time since I'd had a clear thought. Instead, I was staring at the Steps and Traditions on the wall. And my "clear" thought was this: "What on earth does that *mean?*" I read the Steps over and over, trying to make sense of them. The only thing I could finally sort out was this: they were talking about God, and I wanted no part of it. I left the meeting more discouraged than when I'd walked in.

I had nothing personal against God or a Higher Power. Hadn't I prayed? And prayed and *prayed*, for help, for sobriety, for sanity? Hadn't I prayed every day that this would be the day I'd put the bottle down, and the world would come into focus before my eyes, and I'd finally be able to manage my life and my wayward mind? Hadn't I prayed, too, that my mental illness would disappear? Hadn't I sat night after night with my drink and my foxhole prayers, trying to believe that I could drink myself sane—or at least drink myself into oblivion and out of the pain I was in?

Talk about doing things backward. Every day I did just what I needed to do to keep myself in misery: I drank. At night I tossed my meds back with a drink and wondered why on earth they weren't working. Who cared if every single doctor I'd ever seen told me *not to drink on my meds?* They were just saying that, I was sure. They didn't know what they were talking about. If they had my life, I thought, they'd drink too. If they had to live with a mental illness, they'd be drinking with the best of them.

That's probably the biggest fallacy about mental illness and addiction: that we use because the pain of our mental illness "makes" us use. The pain we're in (so the theory goes) "makes" us reach for the substances we abuse. We are (we've all heard it) "self-medicating."

Well, so are all the other addicts. They're in pain too. What sobriety helps us understand is that we don't really drink because we're in pain. We drink because we're addicts. And that in itself is pain enough.

I drank when my mental illness was painful, sure. And I drank when it wasn't. I drank when I was stable, unstable, happy, sad. I drank to celebrate, and I drank to wallow in my sorrows. I drank because it was Tuesday, because it was sunny, because it was raining, but most of all, I drank *because I'm a drunk*.

The element of truth to the idea that mental illness causes us to self-medicate is this: people who have mental illness are highly pre-disposed to *also* have the mental illness of addiction. This isn't a psy-chological correlation, it's a physical one. People who are born with a genetic predisposition to mental illness are also born with a good chance of becoming addicts. Nearly half of people with depression, more than half of people with bipolar disorder, and many people with schizophrenia and other mental disorders deal with substance abuse at some point in their lives. Those of us with mental illness in our family tree often also have alcoholism and other addictions in-scribed on our genes. There seems to be a close genetic relationship between the mental illness of addiction and other mental illnesses.

This means that we're born with a double whammy waiting for us. And when we get hit, we get hit hard. Addicts with mental illness have lower rates of recovery than addicts without. But that doesn't mean we can't get sober. We absolutely can. As it says in the Big Book, "even people with grave emotional and mental disorders can recover if they have the capacity to be honest." We have that capacity. But like other addicts, we have to dig deep to find the honesty with ourselves that we need to find sobriety. That honesty is one of the elements of sanity that we'll recover as we move through the Steps and as we work Step Two.

So how *do* we define sanity? When I was in early recovery, I spent a lot of time trying to explain to my sponsor that I couldn't be *restored* to sanity if I'd never *had* it. And I believed I had not. I believed my mental illness had been the cause of all the insanity in my life. I didn't see yet how insane I'd been in my addiction. I even doubted, in some secret part of myself, if I really needed to get sober. Maybe, I thought, if I just get my mental illness under control, then I can keep drinking. Maybe if I just get on the right meds, get the right therapist and psychiatrist, do all the *other* things they're telling me I need to do—*then* can I drink?

And *that* is the insanity of addiction. It didn't seem to matter how far from sanity I'd fallen through my chemical use. I could still talk myself into believing that the *real* problem was my mental illness. I could persuade myself that if my mental illness was magically eradicated, I'd be free to drink like a gentleman.

Every addict is living in insanity. Not just those of us with mental illness. But those of us with mental illness need to see how our addiction itself has made us insane, and see how we need to deal with that separately from our mental illness, before we have any hope of sanity at all. This is a plain fact: *until we stop using, we have no hope of managing our mental disorders.*

There are many, many ways in which active addiction creates utter insanity in our lives. The most obvious of these, and the first that has to be dealt with, is the way in which we are physically affected by chemicals and the way they massively exacerbate our mental ill-

ness. Many of us, when we are using, are utterly baffled by this relationship between even casual chemical use—let alone our addictive
abuse—and a worsening in our mental illness. What happened? we
wonder, after a night of partying is followed by a crisis in our mental health. They seem unrelated. Why would a few glasses of wine
(or a few bottles) catapult us into mental health mayhem? Well, because that's how our brain chemistry works. We just can't use—it's
as simple as that. Even people with mental illness who use "socially"
feel the negative effects of their use. And those of us who use abu-
sively feel the major damage our using does.

How does that damage play out? We've all felt the morning-after
despair, that pit in the stomach as we try to remember what happened the night, or days or weeks, before. We cringe at things we
said and did. We look around at the mess in our homes and lives
and feel the despair at having to put it all back together again—
we wonder if we even can. We wonder why it happened, why we
couldn't just have a few and call it good like the rest of our peers.
What's wrong with me? we wonder. And those are things that all
addicts have felt and will feel until they sober up. One of the great
gifts of sobriety is waking up in the morning without that sense of
debilitating dread and shame. Waking up free and light of spirit is
an amazing feeling, and as we move through the Steps, we feel it
more and more.

But for those of us with mental illness, the morning and days after
when we're still using are filled not just with those typical addict's
feelings. They're filled with things like violent mood swings, deep de-
pressions, devastating manias, paranoia, anxiety, obsessive thoughts,
and more. The symptoms of our mental illnesses get drastically
worse and come at us fast and furious as we scramble to hang on to
our sanity—and can't. This is the kind of insanity of addiction that
we know all too well.

We are not to blame for our mental illnesses. But we are responsible for doing all we can to manage them. Similarly, we are not at fault for having been born with a predisposition to addiction. But we are responsible for staying sober so that we can prevent the kind of damage we do and the insanity we create when we are using.

It's important to be aware, here, that there is a subtle difference between the kind of instability our mental disorders cause us, and the kind of insanity that our substance abuse brings on. There are times, even when we're sober and taking real care of our health, when our mental illness disrupts our sanity, influences our choices, and causes us to act in ways that are not rational or healthy. This lack of stability is not always something we can control. That's something we have to accept: we are not always masters of our own minds.

But we are in a position to do all we can to maximize our mental health, to increase the time between episodes of illness, and to mitigate the symptoms of illness when they do occur. One of the ways we can do this is to keep our bodies free of substances that exacerbate the symptoms of our mental disorders every time we use them. It is one thing to acknowledge that our disorders may cause us to act out in unhealthy ways; knowing that, we are able to prevent it as much as possible and to repair problems when they do occur. But it is quite another to blame acting out on our mental illnesses when it is in fact a result of our addictive behavior.

We are and should be held accountable for our actions. There are times when those actions are influenced by our mental illnesses; on occasion, we may act in ways that we didn't mean to and would not have if we could have helped it. Despite the fact that we are not responsible for *having* a mental illness, we may need to occasionally repair damage done. We do not always have control over our actions when our mental illness is active. But we *do* have control over whether or not we choose to manage our mental health to the best of our ability. And we do have control over whether we choose to recover from our addictions. We are accountable for that choice.

Plain and simple: even a very small amount of drugs or alcohol in our system worsens our mental illness. Our meds don't work when we're using. Our moods and minds are put in chaos. Our perception is altered more dramatically when we use than the perception of a person without mental illness who uses. With that altered perception, things get cloudy—we can't think straight, and all clarity of thought is lost.

And to use when that happens to us over and over again is insanity as well. Many of us already know that our use exacerbates the symptoms of our mental illness, and yet we just can't seem to put the bottle down. This causes a degree of despair that's almost hard to put into words. And this is one of the hardest aspects of being a person with a mental illness and with the mental illness of addiction at the same time: the insanity of addiction makes it impossible to gain any stability or sanity in our lives; and, worse, it strips us of the faith that stability and sanity will ever be *possible* for us. We are caught in a devastating loop of addictive use, loss of sanity, and despair that sanity won't ever be ours.

Then how can we believe that a Power greater than ourselves can restore us to sanity?

This is the "God problem" many addicts have with the Twelve Steps. And it *can* be a problem—because we often make it so. Some of us approach the idea of God or a Higher Power with little to no difficulty, and those people have less trouble swallowing the idea that they'll need to develop some kind of spiritual life in order to feel the full effects of sobriety. But others have an immediate and powerful negative reaction to the suggestion that a Higher Power needs to play any role in our sobriety or our lives.

We often see the word *God* in the Steps on the wall and hightail it out of the meeting as fast as we can. Then we claim to know all we need to know about the program, and what we claim to know is that it's a religious organization like all the others we don't buy. I've spent more time talking sponsees and newcomers down off the wall about this idea than I can even remember, just as I had to get talked down when I came to the program myself.

But all of us have reasons for our reaction to the idea of a Higher Power. We come at the concept with everything from incredulity to fear to rage. We come at it with whole histories of thinking about God (the existence or absence or nature of such a being) and about religion (the goodness, badness, truth, or falseness of it). We come with a lifetime of experiences, both internal and external, with spirituality and religion as well. No question about it—God, a Higher Power, and spirituality are all loaded concepts, and it's no wonder we have such varied and often problematic reactions to the notion that spirituality will play a role in our recovery.

The first thing to get out of the way is this: Religion has nothing to do with it. The Twelve Steps are *not* a religious program. You don't have to believe in a religious God to get sober. You don't have to agree with any religious ideas or claims. You don't have to join any religious body or practice any religion at all. All you need, as it says in the Big Book, is an open mind.

Here's what that book has to say on the matter:

> Most emphatically we wish to say that any alcoholic capable of honestly facing his problems . . . can recover, provided he does

not close his mind to all spiritual concepts. He can only be defeated by an attitude of intolerance or belligerent denial.

We find that no one need have difficulty with the spirituality of the program. *Willingness, honesty and open-mindedness are the essentials of recovery. But these are indispensable.*

And as Herbert Spencer writes, quoted in the Big Book: "There is a principle which is a bar against all information, which is proof against all arguments and which cannot fail to keep a man in everlasting ignorance—that principle is contempt prior to investigation."

I came to the question of a Higher Power with just that: contempt, and a tightly closed mind. I couldn't see how a Higher Power *wasn't* related to religion. And I had plenty of opinions about religion. I was pretty sure it was the source of many, if not most, of the evils in the world. And let's face it, religion has plenty of drawbacks and has been the source of a whole lot of conflict in the history of time. But my opinions on the matter had precious little foundation. Furthermore, my belief that a Higher Power and religion were inseparable was simply without basis. Still, wresting my *feelings* about spirituality from my *opinions* about religion took some doing.

In truth, I didn't really know what spirituality was. I didn't have a concept of *spirit*. I didn't know what mine felt like—until I really started looking, with as open a mind as I could muster, at my own internal life. And what I found, looking at the years I'd spent in the insanity of addiction, was that my spirit was sorely in need of sustenance. What did I have left, as an inner life? I'd starved my spirit nearly to death in my addiction—given it no faith, denied it all forms of grace. And I'm not talking about religion. I'm talking about the spiritual sustenance that comes from caring relationships with others, fulfilling emotional experiences, wonder at the goodness of the world. These are things that feed the soul. And I had not fed mine in years. My spirit was a pale shadow of what a spiritually alive person's should be. It got that way through years of deprivation and abuse. When I came to sobriety, I realized that the reason I was so suspicious of spirituality was that my spirit felt like it was dying, or dead.

The idea of faith was new to me. Not necessarily faith in a religious God, though that works for many people. Faith in the spiritual grace that I have found in sobriety.

The way I got here was circuitous and meandering. But it has worked. Many—probably most—people in sobriety get to a spiritual life and a relationship with some form of a Higher Power in that same way. The Big Book, in its original form, struck many readers as far too concerned with a religious God. That's why the appendix on "Spiritual Experience" was added (quoted above). In that section, they talk about the fact that many spiritual experiences are of what William James calls the "educational variety," which take place over time, rather than of the lightning-bolt variety, which happen all at once and are pretty rare. Let's face it—few of us change overnight. Spirituality doesn't happen overnight, either, and we can't expect it to, but that's why all we need is an open mind.

Here's that appendix again, on what spiritual experience sometimes looks like:

> Quite often friends of the newcomer are aware of the differ-
> ence long before he is himself. He finally realizes that he has
> undergone a profound alteration in his reaction to life; that
> such a change could hardly have been brought about by him-
> self alone. What often takes place in a few months could sel-
> dom have been accomplished by years of self-discipline. With

few exceptions our members find that they have tapped an unsuspected inner resource which they presently identify with their own conception of a Power greater than themselves.

So if "such a change could hardly have been brought about by [ourselves] alone," what or who is bringing it about? That's entirely up to you to figure out, because with sobriety that change will come, and only you can determine what causes it. I figure that there are a whole lot of things in the universe that are more powerful than I am, and any one of them will do. Any number of things have influenced the change that's come about in me—meetings, other sober people, my sponsor, service work, working the Steps themselves, to name just a few. And that's not even considering the role a "God" might play in my spiritual life. The point is that my *spirit* has come to life, and there are a great many things that feed it and keep it healthy and alive.

There's also the tendency to think that "spiritual experience" has to be a single, dramatic event. That's not what happened to me, and it's not common among the sober people I know. What happened to me was this: I stopped being mad. Let me explain. When I was still using—in fact, for my entire life—I'd been in a rage. At everyone and everything, but most of all at myself. In fact, when I was early in sobriety, I was worried that I'd *stop* being mad. I worried that I'd "lose my edge," but what really bothered me was the idea that I'd stop being the one thing I'd always been: mad. Furious. Insane with anger. Sick with it. Exactly: I was spiritually sick, and anger was poisoning me, even though it was the one thing about me I knew to be true.

And then, years into sobriety, it dawned on me one day: I wasn't mad. Hadn't been mad for as long as I could remember. I was—I could hardly believe it—*at peace*. With myself, with the people around me, with the world. I realized that I'd had a spiritual experience: a change had come about in me that I could never have forced on my own, no matter how much self-will I applied to it; and that change in me was so profound that it had lifted an enormous burden, a burden I didn't even know I was carrying, but that had nearly crushed my spirit completely. And that burden was gone.

The world I lived in was no different. The people around me were the same. What had changed was the way I saw them, the way I experienced them, and the way I experienced my life. What had changed was indefinable; it was a spiritual change. And it brought me what I had always craved: that inner peace. That *peace of mind.*

And that, to me, is sanity. My mental illness is still there, certainly. But I have come to believe that a Power greater than myself can, and does, and will restore me to the sanity I've found—the sanity of freedom from the despair of addiction, the sanity of mental health not constantly destabilized by chemicals, and also the sanity of peace of mind. The Power that feeds our spirit and leads to serenity doesn't have to be explicitly defined or even clearly understood. It works in us regardless; it has worked in the millions of lives of people who've found sobriety. It has restored sanity to those people, whether they have a mental illness or not, and it will restore sanity to you. All that is required is an open mind; that open mind is a door through which serenity can come.

What Step Two gives us, ultimately, is hope. In Step One, we felt the despair of defeat; now, in Step Two, we can rest assured that there is hope for us and for our recovery. Knowing that we will be restored to sanity as we work the Steps, we are ready to move on to the spiritual challenge of Step Three.

Surrender

*Made a decision to turn our will and our lives
over to the care of God* as we understood Him.

FOLLOWING ON THE HEELS OF TWO OPPORTUNITIES for reflection—Step
One, where we finally became honest enough with ourselves to recognize that we were powerless over our drug of choice and that our lives
were out of control; and Step Two, where we came to recognize that
faith in a Power greater than ourselves is necessary and will bring us
to a place of sanity—Step Three requires an act: we must *decide.*

This sounds like a simple enough act, but this decision we're making
is a crucial one, and our sobriety and sanity depend upon it. Unless
we take this Step seriously, our efforts to take the Steps that follow it
will be in vain, because in this Step we discover in ourselves things
we will need for the rest of our journey: willingness, acceptance,
and belief.

But all we need to take this Step is one of those things: willingness.
From willingness follow the gifts of acceptance and belief—it's willingness that shows us those results. We don't need to have a thorough
understanding of our Higher Power to take Step Three; we don't
even need to believe in one. All we need is willingness. Are you *willing*
to learn a new way of living? Are you *willing* to turn your life over to
the care of something greater than yourself?

OK, no. Maybe not. I certainly wasn't when I first stared this Step in the face, and I'd venture a guess that most addicts approaching the overwhelming prospect of letting go of all the illusions they hold dear, most notably the illusion that they are running their own lives, are about as baffled, frightened, and frankly unhappy about it as I was. You'll find at meetings that people often laugh at how scared they were of Step Three when they first got there. Many of us manage to make it through Step Two—which was hard enough—and find ourselves face-to-face with what seems like an absolutely insurmountable task: letting go.

Who knew that letting go would be so hard? Who knew we were clinging so desperately to the idea of our own independence, our own self-sufficiency, our own capacity to run our lives? I for one had run my life right into the ground, no question about it. I knew that. But when I was asked to turn over my will to a Higher Power, my first response was, more or less, *Hell, no.*

Not many people sail straight through Step Three with no effort at all. Most of us are stubborn, and most of us are afraid. But what extra challenges does this Step pose for people with mental illness— and what extra gifts might it bring?

In my experience, and in the stories I've heard from other addicts with mental illness, the first stumbling block we reached was delusion— the delusion that we could, through sheer force of will, *make* our mental illness go away, *make* our addiction go away, and *force* our lives under our control. My fondest belief, long held and without basis, was that if I just *tried hard enough*, I'd think like other people, drink like other people, and be like other people—or at least be as calm, cool, and collected as they all seemed to be. If I just kept trying, I'd be as *in control* of myself, my life, and the world as those people were.

Where did I come up with this stuff? Well, apparently I wasn't alone in it. Turns out that addicts as a bunch are possessed of the notion that a bulldozing approach to life is the best one—and it turns out, too, that it has gotten all of us into the same mess. From the *Twelve Steps and Twelve Traditions:* "Our whole trouble had been the misuse of willpower. We had tried to bombard our problems with it instead of attempting to bring it into agreement with God's intention for us."

But for those of us who deal with mental illness, the illusion of control can be especially appealing. When we so often feel that our lives and our minds themselves are *beyond* our control, the first instinct we have is to try to wrest them back *under* control. We try this and try this, over and over, for years, each time becoming more frustrated and more bewildered by our "failure" to do the impossible—run our lives on self-will alone—and each time becoming more firmly convinced that we just need to try harder. In other words, with every attempt to force ourselves into sobriety and sanity by sheer willpower, and each failure that followed, we redoubled our commitment to the delusion that we're in control.

The revelation that we are not, in fact, running the show is not an immediately comforting or comfortable one. I felt like I was in total free fall when informed that I wasn't the one running my life. Well, I demanded, if I wasn't, who was?

My sponsor pointed out, somewhat sarcastically, that the world also did not turn because I told it to turn. I half-believed it did. And I seriously questioned the wisdom of turning my life over to whatever force turned the world; that force seemed far too big to have much concern with a life as small and wrecked as mine. She asked how it was working out for me to run my own life. I had to agree that it wasn't going all too well. So, she said, turn it over. Act. *Make the decision* to turn your life and your will over to the care of God *as you understand Him.*

Well, I didn't understand Him, It, or They. I couldn't make the leap of faith that if I trusted It, It would run my life well if I turned it over. Talk about arrogance. I was pretty sure that if there was a God, he was bound to mess up my life if I let him. And so I took the advice of all the people in the program: they told me, simply, *Do the next right thing.* And the difference between *doing God's will* and *doing the next right thing* isn't all that great. It is a difference in how we see a Higher Power, and we are free to see that as we choose.

Some people find it useful to think of turning themselves over to the program, to their group, or to working the Steps. These are concrete, practical things that require our willingness. We have evidence of their effectiveness in the other people in the program who are living the kind of lives we ourselves want to lead—we see their sanity, serenity, and sobriety, and we want it. Turning ourselves over to the program and the Steps is a viable way of practicing willingness, and it has worked for millions of sober people.

What I discovered was that the *willingness* to let go of the reins, to let go of the notion that my ideas of how to run my life were the right ones, was enough. I became willing to entertain the radical idea that I was not in charge. And that willingness made all the difference: it led to acceptance and belief.

At first I heard the word *acceptance* as a synonym for *letting yourself be run over by the world and other people.* That's not what it means. Acceptance is a form of peace. Acceptance is the maturity and willingness to see and appreciate the world as it is, without trying to manipulate or control it; it is the ability to let go of the delusion of control altogether. Acceptance allows us to greet *life on life's terms.* And that ability is a source, paradoxically, of enormous strength.

And, like many people, I first heard the word *belief* as *belief in a religious God.* That's one of many possible meanings, but not the only one. Some people, upon making a decision to turn their will and their lives over, do feel a greater understanding of such a God. Many others feel that they have finally been admitted entrance into the human race; for them, the belief that is found is a connection to the people around them, from whom they'd been terribly isolated for so long. Ultimately, *belief* results from willingness, from turning over our will. When we believe, we are willing to take a leap of faith, to make the effort; the effort has concrete results, and these are proof, and this strengthens our belief. With Step Three, we are given a peaceful knowledge that we are all right and our lives will proceed as they should, if we just keep letting go.

Willpower, willingness—the question of the human will is clearly a big one, and the resistance to letting go is a decidedly ordinary human trait. We all do it. We're encouraged by the world we live in to see ourselves as masters of our little universe, and we're designed with an ego that seems to have been provided to us mostly for the purposes of overcoming it. There is a difference between a healthy, stable sense of self and self-worth, on the one hand, and real arrogance or egotism, on the other. When our ego is overblown, it must be brought back down to right size. When it's running the show, it can keep us trapped in ourselves when what we most need is connection to others and to a source of spiritual sustenance. Overblown ego is what fears disintegration if we turn over our will and our lives to a force larger than ourselves. That ego says: if I turn over those things—in which I've had so much faith, however misguided that faith may have been—what will become of *me*?

Take an example straight from the lives of many people with mental illness: medication. Let's be clear: I'm talking about psychiatric medications that balance neurochemistry, bring reality into focus, and allow us to function, as opposed to mood-altering substances designed to distort reality. It's important that we remember that taking our medication is part of our health care management and supports our sobriety; it does not mean we are "using."

But many of us have been unwilling to believe in the necessity of medication for the management of our illness. We have turned a blind eye to the enormous body of science that supports the facts that (a) our brains are wired differently than the average brain; (b) our brain chemistry can cause imbalance in our moods, thoughts, and lives; and (c) that imbalance can be stabilized and our moods, thoughts, and lives made more manageable by medications that science has produced.

We have been slow to recognize reality: first, we are slow to recognize that we have an illness, and next, we are reluctant to realize that there is help for us. Why is this? Well, we live in a world that still holds antiquated, unscientific notions about the brain and how it works. Many people, including people with mental illness, feel certain that our struggle comes from a failure of character or is a negative trait of personality, rather than acknowledging the simple scientific truth: that brain diseases, or mental illnesses, do exist and profoundly affect the daily lives of those who have them.

If we can't see or accept that we have an illness, then we can't believe in the usefulness of medication to treat it. But many of us have already beat our heads against that particular wall long enough, and have come to accept both our illness and the medication that helps us. We know perfectly well that without our meds, many of us would be functioning at a much lower level, if at all. That's a fact that irks us, sure, but we can see the sense of acceptance rather than resistance. So, in that area of our lives, we are willing to allow that we are dependent, in some ways, on science to stabilize us.

Of course, those of us who deal with both the mental illness of addiction and another mental health diagnosis are in particularly bad shape, because even when we are willing to admit that medication *might* help, we are often consuming substances or acting in ways that completely nullify the benefits those medications might have. So we're between a rock and a hard place. But as we put down our drug of choice and make our journey through the Steps, we begin to see that an acceptance of certain forms of dependence is necessary and that it is an opportunity for growth. We are not reduced to a childish state of neediness when we accept our dependence; instead, we are taking on a much-needed dose of maturity.

The absence of maturity, in this sense, is fatal: if we choose a suicidal dependence upon substances that are killing us, physically and spiritually, over a healthy dependence upon a Higher Power, the Twelve Step program, and the wiser people in our lives, we will stay sick. We will continue rattling the cage of our addiction and untreated mental illness, when all along we are free to open the door and step out into the world. And in that cage ultimately we will die.

What is this absence of maturity? It is what keeps us convinced that our addiction isn't so bad, that our mental illness doesn't exist or doesn't need responsible care; it is what keeps us convinced that if we try hard enough, we will "fix it" using the power of willpower alone, independent of any number of sources of healthy assistance; it is what tells us we are "hurting no one but ourselves," because we are blind to how we affect the people around us; it is what tells us, ultimately, that we are in control and that no one can tell us how to live.

The absence of maturity can otherwise be understood as the trap of self. The Big Book puts it rather plainly:

> Selfishness—self-centeredness! That, we think, is the root of our troubles. Driven by a hundred forms of fear, self-delusion, self-seeking, and self-pity, we step on the toes of our fellows and they retaliate. Sometimes they hurt us, seemingly without provocation, but we invariably find that at some time in the past we have *made decisions based on self* which later placed us in a position to be hurt. . . . The [addict] is an extreme example of self-will run riot.

Those decisions—the ones based on self—are the opposing force that runs directly counter to the decision we must make in Step Three. Based in self and living out of fear, we make the decision to cling to our illusion that we are in control, but the decision we are being asked to make, to let go of that illusion, is one based in our spiritual life and requires a bravery we may feel we do not have. But we *do* have it. As the millions of people in recovery who have taken Step Three will tell you, this is a matter of that dread word: *surrender.*

Speaking for myself, the suggestion that I lacked maturity when I came into the program sent me into a rage. How *dare* these people suggest that I was immature. I was a worldly person, or rather grandly imagined myself to be so; I had lived independently (if you don't count my constant companion, the bottle) for many years; I had done all manner of things that I supposed were proof of my maturity. I was able to ignore the inconvenient fact that my untreated mental illness absolutely debilitated me—and made me completely dependent upon others—on a regular basis, because I refused to treat it responsibly; I also ignored the fact that my using life had brought me to my knees because I was unable to admit the plain fact that I was clearly *not* in control.

It was explained to me that the lack of maturity I suffered from was not the sort of obvious immaturity I was thinking it was (though I had plenty of that as well); it was the immaturity of the overdeveloped brain and the undeveloped spirit. I needed to attain both a practical and a spiritual maturity if I ever hoped to find my way out of the hell of untreated mental illness and active addiction.

A few years into sobriety, I got hit with a serious episode of my mental illness. It absolutely took me out. Very suddenly, I was unable to work, unable to function in almost any way. I spent most of my time in the psych ward; when I was home, I needed people to help me with even basic tasks. I didn't know how long it was going to last; in the end, it lasted more than two years.

It was hellish. And I know that if I had not been sober, there is no way I could have accepted what was going on. I could not have turned to the people in my life and, without shame, asked them for help. I could not have found the measure of peace that I did find, even as my mental illness raged. I could not have listened to the doctors when they told me to hang on to hope.

It was the spiritual and emotional growth that I came to through sobriety that allowed me to surrender—not to give up but to accept that situation, to acknowledge that my mental illness required full-time care, and to deal with the fact that other things had to be set aside for a while. Had I fought the reality of the situation, I would have only gotten sicker and suffered more. Instead, sobriety showed me that I had the emotional and spiritual tools to handle even the things I dreaded most.

Surrender is what we must do if we are to practice these Twelve Steps, if we are to be restored to sanity, and if we are to achieve any measure of serenity. In taking these Steps, we are promised "a new freedom and a new happiness," and we will reach those only through surrender. Step Three is where we first find ourselves at the doorstep of that freedom. Here we are given the opportunity to hand over the great burden of our illusions to a Power greater than our *self*—however we choose to understand that Power. All we have to understand is that there *is* something vastly greater than self, there is a world with which we must connect, there is a spiritual life we must begin, in whatever way we can. As we surrender to the welcome reality that *we are not alone*, we finally connect with that larger something, and the great weight of our isolation and fear begins to lift.

It is willingness that allows us to surrender, and it is surrender that leads us to faith. The trap of self falls away, and we are able to see that we are part of an intricate web of humanity and spirit, from which we draw our strength and to which we are responsible. Although we initially thought that Step Three was asking us to erase ourselves by turning over control, we now find that the Step actually brings us to a greater knowledge of ourselves. In practicing Step Three, as we try to bring our will in line with God's will or try simply to do the next right thing, we are constantly examining our core values. These values have long been obscured by our fear and our superficial selves. But in Step Three, we are able to brush away the dust and grime of illusion to discover what we truly believe.

Mental illness and addiction can be so all-consuming that when we find ourselves on the doorstep of recovery, we aren't sure anymore who we really are or what we believe. I was so used to my desperate scramble just to get from day to day that I was deeply buried in a consciousness only of my own needs, my own wishes, my own failures, and my own demands. That's natural enough; pain and struggle suck you into yourself, away from the human and spiritual world. Far from trying to align myself with the will of a Higher Power or even from trying to do what I believed was right, I had gotten stuck in a loop of trying to figure out how to save myself at all costs. I had no consciousness of my impact on others or the world; I had no awareness of how my daily mayhem trapped me in my ego and separated me from others, from spirit, and even from my true self. I prayed, without much faith, that my mental illness would be magically cured, and prayed that God would stop me from drinking, as if he'd reach down and take the bottle right out of my hand. I prayed that I'd be kept safe, when I put myself directly in harm's way; I prayed for things to go better for me, despite my refusal to do the things required for that to happen; I prayed that the people I was damaging wouldn't leave me; I prayed that all would be made well, when I wasn't willing to do a thing to make it so.

In short, I wasn't praying; I was demanding, negotiating, wheedling, whining, and wishing. I wasn't giving over my will to a Power greater than myself; I was telling the powers that be how to serve me best. I was all self-will, no surrender. And I stayed stuck, and sick.

Surrender was the only choice if I wanted health and peace of mind. I could always make the choice to climb back in the cage of self. But the peace of mind found through willingness and surrender is vastly preferable to that old willful trap. The freedom made possible by Step Three brings us our first real taste of serenity.

And for those of us with mental illness, this Step allows us to begin learning, or to deepen, our acceptance of the facts of our lives. With Step Three, as we let go of the impulse to control everything, we are able to recognize that our mental illness does not respond to willpower, to attempts to "fix it," or to head-in-the-sand pretending it isn't there.

So we begin to approach our mental health in a very practical, non-fearful way; we learn to accept it and therefore to manage it so that we can be our most functional selves. This ability to face our circumstances without fear, self-pity, or blame is liberating. And the fact that we are consistently managing our mental illness means we become more effective at controlling its day-to-day symptoms: by not avoiding the reality of our mental disorders, we are better able to manage feelings and thoughts that would otherwise have controlled us.

No longer operating in a state of "self-will run riot," we are also able to halt the dangerous, counterproductive behaviors that prevent us from managing our illness. We can finally hear and apply a proactive approach to management, making the changes in the way we live and treat our health that will bring us to a state of greater stability. By applying the acceptance I'd learned in Step Three, I was finally able to develop a plan for managing my mental health that actually *works*, where all my attempts to "control" it had failed.

We also approach a greater state of balance in thinking about our mental health. We begin to see how we must balance between, on the one hand, dependence upon the support of people and, in many cases, medications and, on the other, the greater independence that comes from taking responsibility for our health and ourselves. For so long we've seen dependence as failure, and independence as a state of total self-sufficiency. This is the all-or-nothing thinking that addicts are so prone to. But Step Three teaches us what healthy dependence and healthy independence really are.

Self-will is a form of fear, while willingness is a form of faith. As we take the leap of faith that is Step Three, we find that we are not in free fall after all; we land on solid ground and find ourselves standing on the strong foundation of the Steps. Step Three has freed us from the trap of ego and delusion and given us instead the gift of acceptance and the wisdom of surrender. No longer clinging to our old ideas, we are free to move forward on our journey toward seren-ity. The decision we made in Step Three—to turn over our will and our lives—has freed us to do the mental, spiritual, and emotional housecleaning we'll do in Step Four.

Honesty

Made a searching and fearless
moral inventory of ourselves.

STEP THREE LIFTED AN ENORMOUS BURDEN from us, the burden of the delusion that we are always in control. With this burden gone, we can breathe a little easier—and we can get on with our work on the Steps.

The Fourth Step is the one most people slog toward with dread and trepidation, dragging their feet and grumbling (or kicking and screaming). Some people make it through Step Three, then see Step Four coming and pitch the whole idea of sobriety right out the window. Others tell themselves they can leap over Steps Four and Five and start again at Step Six—anything so long as they don't have to do a Fourth Step. It's actually pretty funny, the image of millions of newcomers staring in horror at a blank piece of paper. Except that if you're the one doing the staring, it's not funny at all.

This Step poses some special challenges for a person with mental illness, but it also offers great rewards. We are particularly adept at finding reasons to be angry with ourselves, and we are not particularly adept at finding balance in our self-assessment. We often vacillate wildly between self-hatred and self-pity, feeling sometimes that we are to blame for all the things that go wrong in our lives and our minds, and, alternately, that everyone and everything else are the root cause of our pain. In reality, this is not an either/or proposition. Our troubles stem from a whole lot of things. We can't change them all. We can't change other people. We can't change the fact that we have a mental illness. The one thing we can change is our approach to life—to those other people, to our mental illness, and to who we are. But in order to do that, we need to take stock.

The very suggestion that we turn our gaze inward to take an honest look at ourselves can send us reeling with a very real fear of what we're going to see. It isn't news to us that we've made mistakes—all we have to do is take a quick glance at our lives and see how they're littered with empty bottles, lost jobs, alienated friends, estranged family members, and an ever-increasing sense of despair. And it's not news to us that something has to change. But, we say, can't we look forward now instead of dwelling on the past? Can't we just *forget* the past, chalk it up to experience, and turn over a new leaf?

Well, no. We can't. Not just yet. We need to take inventory, no two ways about it. The Big Book compares Step Four to the stocktaking any successful business does now and then, a process by which the business owner assesses what he's got on hand, what's good, what's gone bad, and what he needs to do to make his business more successful going forward. And that *is* what this Step is about: moving forward in our lives. It isn't a matter of dwelling on the past; it's a matter of taking a good hard look at who we are, what we've got, and what we need to develop to live our lives in a new way.

Figuring out how to move forward in our lives, not just as recovering addicts but as people with mental illnesses, can feel like a confounding project. How do we know what's a character defect and what's a symptom? How can we tell when mistakes we've made have been the result of our mental illnesses, and when they've been the result of our addictions? Or neither, or both? How do we know what life looks like as a sober person managing a mental illness when we've never been one? Which aspects of ourselves need healing, which need rooting out, and which are there to stay? What's the difference between a character defect and a character trait? If we stop using and do a Fourth Step, will our mental illnesses go away?

We suspect not, and we're right. At the end of the day, we'll still have mental illnesses, and we'll still have symptoms. Our project is to change those things in ourselves that *can* be changed—the character defects—and accept and do a better job of managing the things that can't—our mental illnesses.

Here's a good opportunity to talk about the Serenity Prayer. This prayer is integral to the fabric of the Twelve Step program, expressing many of the Steps' basic principles in its simple words: *God, grant me the serenity to accept the things I cannot change; the courage to change the things I can; and the wisdom to know the difference.* This prayer helps us practice both acceptance and action, and learn to discern what is required of us in any given situation. With regard to our addictions and mental illnesses, this prayer can help us to accept that we have certain challenges, and to take action to manage them well.

Doing a Fourth Step didn't cure my mental illness, as convenient as that would have been. It didn't magically take away the things about me that are just sort of crummy. I didn't become a perfect person overnight, and it looks like I'm not going to. But making a thorough and honest inventory *did* give me a clear-eyed view of what makes me tick, where I've been, and what has led to the choices I've made. With that knowledge, I am able to develop a whole set of tools to manage my mental illness, my addiction, and my life.

Step Four is about honesty, accountability, and humility. For us, the old maxim "Know thyself" is an important one. We do need to know ourselves if we want to take charge of our lives. For so long, we have done nothing but react, usually destructively, to powerful forces within and without ourselves. With Step Four, we begin to live proactively, making choices rather than swinging blind. Taking this Step, we begin to build the foundation of a peaceful mind and a useful life.

As we begin this Step, the first thing we need to do is drum up some objectivity. If we go charging ahead into the project of self-assessment without it, we're doomed to failure. We'll go in ready to judge, justify, blame, and give up. Those seem like contradictory impulses, but we're all familiar with our tendency to indulge them. Those are, frankly, easy responses to hard news, and sometimes looking at the facts about ourselves and our lives gives us hard news. The more challenging and utterly necessary response is one of equanimity, of balance. As we dig through the rubble of self and life, we need to be ready to see whatever we see, without judgment, justification, or blame. We need to be ready to persevere, whatever we learn. We need to take the same approach we'd take to going through the fridge. This is rotten, this is sour, this is past its freshness date, I can't even tell what this is, and this here is still pretty good.

Simply put, don't take it personally. These are things about yourself, sure. But many of them, even the ugliest, are things you can change as you grow in sobriety. But before you can change them, you need to know they're there, and you need to know exactly what they are and where they come from.

All of this sounded ridiculously complex when I set out to do my Fourth Step. The very suggestion that I look at myself honestly made me scream in anticipatory pain. I explained to my sponsor that it couldn't be done. I said, "What are you thinking? I hate myself enough already." She had quite a time explaining to me that the Fourth Step was not an exercise in self-torture. I heard that I needed humility to work this Step and immediately understood it to mean that I was going to have to relive all the humiliations, small and large, that I was hoping sobriety would bring to a stop. I was not prepared to undergo another onslaught of guilt and sickening self-hatred. And I was loath to spend any more nights lying in bed watching reruns of the mental movie of my mistakes in life.

She finally realized that I didn't know the difference between "humility" and "humiliation." She sighed and said, "Oh, go look it up."

Humiliation: degradation, debasement, dishonor. (See SHAME.)

Humility: the quality or condition of being humble. (Not very helpful.)

Humble: not proud or arrogant; modest. (OK, so . . .)

Modest: having or showing a moderate or humble estimate of one's merits, importance, etc.; free from vanity, egotism, boastfulness, or great pretensions.

Aha! There we go. *Modest. That's* what people were talking about when they said Step Four was about "getting down to right size." And *that* seemed like a totally manageable project. It seemed, actually, like it might be an enormous relief. Instead of living in a grotesque funhouse hall of mirrors, seeing my distorted self first tiny and pathetic, then massive and fearsome, then lowly all over again, I could just look in a mirror and see a *person.* Instead of staggering around under the weight of my own convoluted blend of self-hatred, grandiosity, judgment, and blame, I might be able to walk with a clear conscience and a lighter step. The *Twelve Steps and Twelve Traditions* agreed with me: when we take inventory, it says, "a wonderful light falls upon this foggy scene. As we persist, a brand-new kind of confidence is born, and *the sense of relief at finally facing ourselves is indescribable*" (emphasis added).

There is no denying that mental illness makes accurate self-perception a very difficult thing to achieve. Perception itself is altered when we're experiencing symptoms, and at those times it can be all but impossible to see ourselves clearly. This is all the more reason to do a Fourth Step. By setting down on paper what we know to be our personal tendencies and patterns, effective and ineffective, we can begin to figure out what are features of our mental illness, and what are traits of our addiction. When we have this in front of us, we have a clear and thorough self-assessment that we can return to when our perception is out of whack. Using our Fourth Step, we are better able to tell when we are experiencing a relapse of our mental illness, and when, instead, we're falling back on the old behaviors and character defects of our addiction.

Here's an example. Two of the symptoms of my mental illness, bipolar disorder, are depression and mania. With depression comes plummeting self-worth, a dark and despairing worldview, and an inability to see hope. With mania often comes grandiosity, a sense of invincibility, and a whole host of dangerous, thrill-seeking behaviors. Trouble is, every one of those things can *also* be a character defect that led to using and can lead there again. Depression can turn into self-pity, grandiosity becomes arrogance, and the general inability to stay *rightsized* is a characteristic of my old using life. So how do I tell when I'm experiencing a simple malfunction of my brain chemistry and slipping into symptoms of bipolar, and when instead I'm reverting to my addict self? How, too, can I assess past behaviors and events with all this in mind?

Tough call. It can be a careful process, picking apart the threads of misinformation we've gotten, misperception we've cultivated, and misguided efforts we've made to control both our use and our mental illness. This is exactly where a Fourth Step comes in.

We need to do this Step under the guidance of our sponsor or therapist. The Big Book has a clear example of one way to do the Fourth Step; there are also a number of good guides that walk you through it. As frightening a prospect as it may seem at first, a thorough inventory is truly essential to working the rest of the Steps and to staying sober. Most of us find that the process was far more liberating than it was painful, and many sober people repeat the process a number of times over the course of the years, discovering new truths and new things to work on each time.

For those of us with mental illness, accurate information is key. At all times, we need knowledge about what our mental illness is, what its symptoms are, and what those symptoms feel and look like in us. If we're laboring under the antiquated notions of mental illness still rampant in our society, and if we hold ourselves hostage to the stigma of mental illness, there is no way we can begin to manage our own. If I believed my mental illness was *itself* a character defect, I'd still be spinning my wheels trying to "root out" that "defect," to no avail, while my addiction and its real defects went unaddressed. So—get that out of the way. Mental illness is a brain disease. But, surprisingly, these Steps can help manage it, and the Fourth Step is one where we learn the facts.

Therefore, we need to read up extensively on our mental illness, ask questions of our doctors and therapists about its symptoms and their triggers, and ask our friends and family members for feedback on how they've seen us behave, think, and feel in the past. This gives us a good foundation for self-assessment. We also need to pay close attention—take notes—to our own experience of symptoms, and begin to see their causes and effects. Once this is done, we have a close knowledge of what our mental illness is and how it makes us feel and behave.

This helps us see where *we* end and *illness* begins. For example, I'm not myself a terribly impulsive person; I don't much like change, and when I'm not symptomatic, I'm a very careful decision maker. But the primary symptom of mania is impulsivity. So when I've been manic, I've made all sorts of wild changes and decisions on little more than a whim, from moving across the country to racking up astronomical debt overnight. Then, when symptoms have been brought under control again, I've been horrified more than once to see the wreckage I've created.

So can I just write off *all* my bad and sudden decisions to my mental illness? Sadly, no. I've also made a whole lot of poor choices when I was drunk, using, or in my addict state of mind, and those have created just as much wreckage in my personal life, if not more. It would be very handy if I could blame my mental illness for every mistake I've made. And, in truth, I've tried. Haven't we all? And wouldn't it be nice if we could blame every unkind word we've said, every unfair thing we've done, every bad situation we've created on the fact that we have mental illness?

Sure. We'd never have to be accountable to anyone or anything. And this Step is, as we've said, all about accountability.

It's hard to understand what "accountable" means when our very minds and emotions are sometimes held hostage to an illness we can't control. How do we stay "accountable" when we're sick?

Very simple: we stay accountable to ourselves and to the people around us *by managing our illness as best we can.* Not when it suits us. All the time. As it says in "How It Works" in the Big Book, "half measures availed us nothing." Taking our medication only when we feel bad is a half measure. Doing the things that we know exacerbate our symptoms are half measures. Using our drug of choice is worse than a half measure—it's a guaranteed disaster.

Skipping the Fourth Step is also a half measure. So let's get on with that.

Once we have a clear idea of what our symptoms are and have made the decision to take responsibility for our own mental health by managing those symptoms to the best of our ability, we can begin to assess the rest. This is where things can get a little uncomfortable. When we begin to recognize that the bulk of our past actions and reactions have been of our own making, a big part of us protests. I, for one, do not much like to think about my character defects; in fact, there's a loud voice in me arguing that "character defects" is a really unpleasant term, and couldn't we use another one, maybe one that makes me sound a little better.

An old-timer once told me a story. He said, "When I first got sober, I just hated the idea that I had what they were calling 'character defects.' I was an arrogant guy, and the idea that I was 'defective' really ticked me off. And so, when I heard someone in a meeting say that his weren't 'character defects,' they were just 'personality traits,' I thought to myself, 'Great! I'm off the hook!'"

"So what happened?" I asked the old-timer.

"I got drunk," he said flatly. "I had to come to grips with the fact that maybe my character was a little less than perfect. So," he said, "this is what an old-timer told *me:* a character defect can be understood as 'that which stands in the way of my usefulness to myself or to others.'"

And that's a really *practical* way of looking at character defects. With that in mind, we don't waste time beating ourselves up about these things; we simply take a proactive approach to changing what needs to be changed. It's the same as looking at our mental illness in an informed, healthy manner: we assess the problem, and we look for the solution.

So we begin our Fourth Step with that in mind: we are working toward a solution for many of the problems that have plagued us throughout our lives. The moral inventory helps us look honestly at those problems and their origins; with that information in hand, we are able to develop solutions and a new way of handling life on life's terms.

In reviewing my own Fourth Steps, and in talking to sponsors and other sober people about theirs, I find the same patterns that the authors of the Big Book found. We may think (as you'll hear people in the program tease) that we're all "terminally unique," but the things that creep up again and again in our inventories are strikingly similar. The ones that knock us down most often are these: resentment, pride, and fear.

"Resentment," according to the Big Book, "is the 'number one' offender. It destroys more alcoholics than anything else. From it stem all forms of spiritual disease."

One of the problems for which many of us need a solution is our tendency not to take responsibility for our lives and our own happiness. This leads to resentment—toward situations, toward our illnesses, toward other people, and even toward ourselves. So much of our past distress has stemmed from the erroneous belief that things can, should, and really *must* go our way if we are to be happy and satisfied. This is a profoundly unrealistic (and pretty immature) way to approach the basic truth that life is challenging, holds difficulty and disappointment, and requires a great deal of effort from us. Our previous pattern was this: we believed that the problem was that life wasn't going our way; our solution was to drink and to resent. The new way of looking at it is this: the problem was our unrealistic expectation that life and other people were responsible for making us happy; the solution is to take responsibility for our own happiness and serenity, whatever life may bring.

As we go through our Fourth Steps, we may see countless instances where our resentments and anger stem from our own expectations rather than from real problems outside ourselves. One by one, we list those resentments, look for their root cause in ourselves, and move on to the next. But one particularly sticky resentment that a lot of people with mental illness are holding on to is their resentment of the illness itself.

And in truth, who can say that it isn't a bum deal? Who among us asked to be sick? Isn't it reasonable that we should be resentful, angry, even enraged at the ways the illness has interfered with our lives?

It is a bum deal. We did not ask to be sick. *But* we do have these illnesses, and we do have to deal with them, and we have found that staying angry, resentful, and enraged just eats us alive. We stay spiritually sick and shut ourselves off from the serenity that could be ours. We also create a fantasy of "normalcy" that doesn't even exist; we tell ourselves that if we had that "normal" life, *then* we'd have serenity. But the truth is that everyone suffers; everyone struggles. Without minimizing the real pain of having mental illness, we must also recognize that millions of others live in equally unfair circumstances—whether they face poverty or trauma, or live in a nation at war—and that each of us, ultimately, must come to grips with the situation we are in.

Acceptance. The problem is not, truly, our mental illness; the problem is our resentment of it, which has led to a million forms of resistance, denial, acting out, refusing to take care of ourselves, blaming it for things that are actually our own responsibility, and allowing ourselves to be dragged down by despair. That is the problem. And the solution is acceptance.

So as we place "mental illness" on our Fourth Step, we take our first step toward ridding ourselves of that resentment. We get down to the bottom of the resentment: what are the thoughts we secretly harbor about our mental illness? Do we feel that life has ripped us off? Do we feel entitled to an easier life? Are we putting off acceptance in the unrealistic expectation that the mental illness will just go away? Who have we hurt in our unhealthy ways of handling our mental illness? How have we hurt ourselves? We place these things on our list, looking objectively at how we've chosen to manage the reality of our lives. And once it's written down in black and white, we begin to let go of this massive resentment and move toward an acceptance that will bring us to serenity.

Pride and fear are other biggies on most people's Fourth Step lists. These feelings, by their very nature, cringe at examination. When we look at our character defects, our pride throws a fit, insisting that we have none, while our fear crawls under the bed, sure that such an examination will destroy us altogether. Once again we're thinking in either/ors. As we push past our initial resistance, we find that a close examination of our lives and selves doesn't kill us. And as we do that examining, we begin to see how pride and fear have cut us off from both our lives and the people in them. We have spent so much time paralyzed with terror of all kinds (fear), and so much time fighting to keep our fragile egos intact (pride) that we have not really lived. Furthermore, we have kept ourselves painfully isolated and alone.

For people with mental illness, facing the twin demons of fear and pride can be particularly rewarding. We have spent so long fearing our own minds, fearing other people, fearing life itself, that when we get sober, we find that we have never fully experienced the joys of life—because we have been afraid. Our pride, too, has cut us off; our ongoing attempts to deny our illness, or hide it, or hide *from* it, have actually held us hostage *to* it. Doing a Fourth Step allows us to see on paper exactly where fear has guided our actions, where pride has harmed us, and how both have kept us very much alone.

Many people say that Step Four was the moment when they regained entrance into the human race. If at first it seems like a solipsistic exercise to do so much self-examination, it turns out in the end to be an exercise of human connection. For self-awareness, born of real honesty and humility, is, paradoxically, the key to creating an empathetic, other-centered life. As we begin to know ourselves, we begin to have insight into the lives, struggles, and needs of others. And as we examine and then let go of our resentments, fears, and other unhealthy traits, we create space in ourselves wherein a spiritual life may freely grow.

The development of empathy and a growing awareness of our way of living in the world are areas of major spiritual growth, as is the exercise of radical honesty that Step Four has required of us. Empathy, awareness of ourselves, and honesty are now put to critical use when we move on to Step Five.

Humility

Admitted to God, to ourselves, and to another human being
the exact nature of our wrongs.

STEP FOUR REQUIRED THAT WE GET SERIOUSLY HONEST with ourselves. And it was hard. But honesty with ourselves isn't enough. If we are going to end our terrible isolation and rebuild our relationship with humanity, we need to get honest with someone else as well. So it's time for Step Five.

This is a Step that strikes fear in the hearts of many recovering people. Many try to skip it, jumping straight from Four to Six, in the sincere hope that they won't have to sit down with another person and actually say, out loud, all the stuff they've kept under lock and key for so long. It's understandable. Sharing our secrets—so many of which we've sworn to ourselves will never pass our lips, so many of which we've tried and tried to forget—is seriously frightening. This is a tough Step.

And I'd venture to say that it's particularly tough for those of us with mental illness. We keep a whole lot of secrets. We've spent lifetimes trying to hide our illness, trying to be someone we're not, and have developed horrible wells of shame about who we are. Our Fourth Steps, if we've been thorough, are not just long but pretty complex; they're written histories of people who've been trying to hide their pain and

51

their reality away from the world for a very long time. We've made mistakes over which we had no control, and we've made mistakes we could have prevented. We blame ourselves for things that aren't our fault, and yet often don't take responsibility for things that are. And many of us have arrived on the doorstep of sobriety carrying such a burden of self-hatred and shame that we can hardly move.

And now the Steps tell us we need to lift the veil on all this. Take off the mask. Tell the truth. All the secrets, all the mistakes, all the sorrows, all the confusion. We have to open Pandora's box while someone else watches.

And a lot of us say, at first, *Not a chance.*

Even though we recognized in doing our Fourth Step that we were practicing humility rather than humiliation, and even though we are beginning to get a handle on the difference between the two, that was back when our secrets were kept between us and a piece of paper. Faced with the requirement that we humble ourselves before another living, breathing—and, we fear, judging—person, we may fear again that we are being asked to humiliate ourselves. It's not true, but we haven't yet learned the real nature of humility or begun to understand its essential and life-giving role in our sobriety. Those of us with mental illness may already have a horrible sense of humiliation in our lives, brought on by our experiences, by social stigma, and by our own self-hatred. And so the idea that we share our histories with someone else sounds like a recipe for a skyrocketing level of shame.

We have to take it on faith: that's not what it is. That's not what will happen. We have to take a deep breath and dive in.

Because one thing I know to be true is this: Step Five is indispensable. Avoid it, and you're heading for a drunk.

In "How It Works," that passage in the Big Book where the Twelve Steps are laid out for the first time, we find these lines: "At some of these [Steps] we balked. We thought we could find an easier, softer way. But we could not. With all the earnestness at our command, we beg of you to be fearless and thorough . . . *Half measures availed us nothing"* (emphasis added).

So here we are: balking at Step Five. Hoping we can find an easier, softer way. Maybe we could just admit to God and ourselves the exact nature of our wrongs and skip the whole part about that other person? Two out of three ain't bad. But in this case, that easier way will keep us sick. It's a half measure. And as we've been told time and again, it will avail us nothing.

Instead, the defects, fears, and resentments we've set down on our Fourth Step will go unspoken and will continue to chase us from place to place and year to year, festering in us and causing shame, anxiety, guilt, remorse, and isolation. Secrets eat away at any addict. For those of us with mental illness, keeping things secret actually exacerbates symptoms of our disorders, deepening depression, heightening anxiety, and feeding into impulsive behavior. The feeling that we should and must keep ourselves and our histories hidden feeds into self-hatred, which leads us to a very dangerous place.

Why do they say the Fifth Step will make such a difference? It seems like skipping just one little Step wouldn't be such a big deal. But the Fifth Step is the one where our commitment to sobriety finds its first real test in the world. Here, sobriety becomes more than just the decision to stay off our substance of choice. This is the first of what are often called the *action steps*—it comes right at the beginning of the Big Book chapter titled "Into Action"—and it takes our decision to take our lives out of the privacy of our hearts and mind and into the world where we live with others. With Step Five, we're changing not just how we *feel* about our addiction, about our mental illness, about a Higher Power, we're changing how we *act*. We begin to impact other people in a new way; we begin to have a new kind of relationship with them. And for that to happen, the Steps set before us this task: we must sit down with one of those people and tell our whole truth.

And if we don't? There will be little to no lasting change in how we live, how we relate to ourselves, our Higher Power, or other people. Our strengths of character will go undeveloped, our weaknesses of character will worsen. We will continue to flounder in the sea of confusion about what makes us do what we do: we will be unable to tell when our actions, both past and present, are driven by mental illness, or by addiction, or by character defect. We will fail to know ourselves well. We will continue to overlook all that is good and strong in ourselves, to see only what is weak and failed, and we will keep lying—to ourselves and to the world.

And it's the dishonesty that sends us straight back into the arms of our addiction and eventually kills us.

There's a line from the Big Book that has always nagged at me. Its message gives me hope, but the way it's said sticks in my craw. It comes from the opening of chapter 5, "How It Works," when the authors are talking about who can get sober and that rarely there are people who cannot "completely give themselves to this simple program." Those who can't recover, they say, are those who are "constitutionally incapable of being honest with themselves." And here's the line that gets to me: "*There are those, too, who suffer from grave emotional and mental disorders, but many of them do recover if they have the capacity to be honest*" (emphasis added).

This is one of the places in recovery literature where my hackles go up: I feel that referring to me and people like me—those of us with mental disorders—as "them" and "they" sets us outside the circle of "real" or "normal" recovering people. But it's an old book, so I give it a pass. Once I get past that, I'm face-to-face with the question that terrified me when I first got sober: *Do* I have the capacity to be honest with myself? *Does* my mental illness mean that I may lack that capacity—and does that mean my mental illness will prevent me from getting sober?

I remember sitting in a midnight meeting when I was in my second round of treatment. It was dark except for the light of a few candles on a low table in the center of the room. People were taking turns sharing about their experience—things they'd done that they felt ashamed of, amends they needed to make, regrets they'd gathered up over their years of using.

I was doing my best to listen as closely as I could to these people. But I was having a hard time connecting. I had just been put on a new medication, the first time I'd been back on meds since I'd gone off them to facilitate my nonstop drinking some years before. The new med was making me dizzy, and I was trying to focus my blurry eyes. And I was trying to focus my attention. But I kept thinking about the afternoon I'd spent with a psychiatrist, who had listened to me try to explain why I didn't need meds, why I didn't need treatment, and why I could probably still drink if I just gave it another try (we've all heard that one, haven't we?).

The psychiatrist had listened carefully and then said to me calmly, "I'll be clear. If you drink again, one of two things will happen. Either you'll go crazy; or you'll go crazy, and then you'll die."

I sat there in his office, trying to let that sink in. I'd been lying to myself for so long, telling myself the drinking wasn't making the mental illness worse, telling myself I wasn't really mentally ill, telling myself

I wasn't really an alcoholic, telling myself I didn't need meds, telling myself anything I wanted to hear—and then believing it.

I said to the psychiatrist that afternoon, "Do you think I'll drink again?" He said, "I don't know. Do you have the capacity to be honest with yourself?"

So I sat there at that midnight meeting, paralyzed with fear, because I had no reason to believe yet that I did have that capacity. I had never been honest with myself. What if I was one of those people, the ones who just weren't able to get sober, because they couldn't face the truth of who they were?

This much I know: for those of us who struggle with the confusion of mental disorders in addition to addiction, the Fifth Step is a lifesaver. If we skip Step Five, we are skipping the cornerstone of our recovery. This cornerstone takes some heavy lifting, but without it, we're on very shaky ground—and most of us, sooner or later, will fall.

Why *is* it so important that we share our Fourth Step with another person, in addition to God and ourselves?

At first glance, this feels like straight-up punishment. It feels like we're being asked to humiliate ourselves by trotting out all our ghosts and demons and ugliness. This unnecessary, if understandable, feeling comes from a couple of sources.

The first is that our self-perception is so distorted that we can only see that ugliness in ourselves, and we desperately fear showing it to someone else. We see our history as a wreckage of one failure after another, one mistake after the next, a chronicle of a ruined person and a ruined life. As we know, this distorted perception of ourselves as particularly awful human beings leads to our constant, often life-long attempt to make people see us as better people than we think we are. The face we show the world and the face we see in the mirror are light-years apart, and we're often desperate to make sure no one else sees the person we see in the mirror. We have gone to radical lengths to seem like someone better, kinder, more generous, more reliable, and—possibly above all else—more *normal* than we really feel. People with mental illness have built especially elaborate facades for themselves and often hide behind a mask of health, stability, and normalcy that they'll do anything to keep intact.

Step Five asks us to put down the mask. And we are terrified of how people will react when they see who we really are. We fear judgment, we fear mocking laughter, we fear horror or disgust—because *those are the things we feel about ourselves.* It is primarily our own distorted self-perception that has kept us locked behind this mask for so long.

When we actually practice Step Five, we find that our worst fears are not realized. We are not the monsters we thought we were. We find that we have an enormous amount in common with other recovering addicts, even those without mental illness. This discovery builds on the tentative feeling we had when we joined our Twelve Step groups and found we weren't the only ones who were so beaten down by our addiction. Step Five takes this a big step further: we realize for the first time that we are not alone in our humanity—flaws, defects, gifts, and all.

Step Five brings an end to the crippling isolation we've felt. Far from an exercise in worsening our shame, it is an exercise in connecting with the world beyond our limited, frightened sense of self. It makes us realize that we are just one addict among many. The sense that we are "terminally unique" can be tossed out, and while we may have had a perverse attachment to our sense of being extraspecially screwed up, it comes as a true relief that we are no worse than anybody else.

I'm willing to bet there are readers who are saying, "But what about my mental illness? Doesn't it mean I am, in some ways, worse off than somebody else? Doesn't it mean my failures are graver, my mistakes more serious, my defects possibly permanent?"

I have said the same things, but I've had to realize that they come from another misperception I held near and dear without even realizing I held it: the perception that mental illness *itself* was a failure, a flaw, a mistake, and a defect. My belief, deep down, was this: the fact that I had a mental illness meant that there was no hope for me—no hope of sobriety, no hope of community, no hope of repairing my ways of living, no hope of an end to isolation—because the mental illness would always keep me hidden, afraid, and alone.

So, to me, it seemed like there was little point in doing Step Five.

Not true.

This is one of the Steps where the challenges to a recovering person with a mental illness are significant, because the Step goes to the core of how we see ourselves as people. And many of us with mental illness see ourselves through a complicated tangle of our own beliefs, society's stigmatizing beliefs, and our interpretations of how our lives have gone. We have conflated symptoms with personal failures, we have blamed our character for things that were actually caused by brain disease, and we have had a hell of a time sorting out *who we are beyond our mental illness.*

But this Step, along with Step Four, can help us clear up that tangled view. If we have been thorough in our Fourth Step, we've made discoveries both powerful and painful. We've begun to develop the ability to discern which events in our past arose from our mental illness and which from our addictive behavior. We've started to identify which aspects of our character are really symptoms of our mental disorder, which are symptoms of our addiction, and which are lasting character defects that need to be changed. We did our best to write down an objective catalog of our resentments, fears, character defects, *and* positive traits. By now we are getting a clearer picture of our history and ourselves. We are beginning to see that we cannot be held responsible for some things and that we must take responsibility for others; we are letting go of those things in ourselves and our lives that can't be changed, and firmly taking charge of the things that can.

So, really, we've already taken a hard look at ourselves, and we've begun to get a more even-eyed view of who we are, where we've been, and where we want to go. What's happening when we hit Step Five and get scared is that when we are faced with telling all this to another person, our old self-hatred and self-doubt kick in, and we forget for a moment the new vision for ourselves we've begun to acquire.

But if we just hang on to that vision, we can bravely sit down with another person and open up to that person. And we will find—as millions of people in Twelve Step programs, mentally ill or not, have done over the years—that our isolation comes to an end.

Isolation, loneliness, and shame—all of them made much worse by our mental illness—these were things that kept us tied to the bottle, to the drug, to whatever substance or behavior kept us trapped for so long. We drank for companionship, we drank to fill up the hunger we felt for closeness and intimacy, we drank to feel "normal," we drank to dull the pain our mental illness caused us in so many ways. For an addict with a mental illness, isolation is not an option. And so we must do whatever it takes to leave that cold and isolated place.

The Fourth Step was a good place to start, but now we must take further action. Our private commitment to sobriety must take on public life. "Until we actually sit down and talk aloud about what we have so long hidden, our willingness to clean house is still largely theoretical," it says in the *Twelve Steps and Twelve Traditions*. That theory must become practice. While we have developed a list of the symptoms and defects that have troubled us, and begun to make a plan of action for managing our mental illness and recovering from our addiction, this list is still a list. We have not yet acquired the full honesty and humility we'll need to live a consistently healthy, sober life.

The practice we are cultivating—the action—is a practice of honesty and humility in all our affairs. *Honesty* becomes easier when we open our stories up to another person in our Fifth Step. Taking this Step, we—many of us for the first time—allow another person to see us without the facade, and having shown our true selves and told our real stories, we gain confidence in our ability to do so day by day. *Humility* becomes possible when we not only recognize our challenges but discuss them with another person.

Opening up like this, no longer hiding who we are or the difficulties we face or the gifts we have to offer, we gradually become used to seeing ourselves as we truly are—neither inflated nor diminished, we become "rightsized." The person we are and the person we seem to be become the same. Only then can we find true stability in our mental health, and only then can we find serenity in recovery.

Becoming rightsized is a process that involves both self-assessment and the assistance of other people in seeing who we are, where we've made mistakes, and how we can change. This is one of the reasons it's so critical that our Fifth Step involve another person. This person, chosen carefully, can give us that all-important guidance and direction that any addict in recovery needs. This is, you've often heard it said, a "we program." Together, *we* help each other by listening and offering our best suggestions. Together, *we* grow by taking direction. Our own best assessment of ourselves, our stories, our situations, and, for those of us who have mental disorders, our symptoms, is not always the most accurate. That's why we need the eyes of another sober person to help us get the clearest view and take the smartest action.

When it's time for us to take the Fifth Step, we choose our listener carefully. For some of us, our sponsor is the best choice. For others, a priest or other spiritual director is more appropriate. For those of us with mental illness, it's imperative that we find someone who understands mental illness well. At all costs, we need to avoid getting misguided advice from a well-meaning sober party who does not understand mental illness or the need for psychiatric medications. For this reason, some of us will do well to choose our therapist or psychiatrist for this important Step. There are many professionals in the fields of psychiatry and psychology who understand recovery, and they can provide excellent guidance and a perspective sensitive to the particular needs and challenges of someone with mental illness. It may take some looking to find the right person, and that's fine—just don't use it as an excuse to put off this important moment in your recovery work.

The Big Book reminds us that when the day comes to give our Fifth Step, we need to pocket our pride. Pride is one of the things that's gotten us into this mess—it's a kind of dishonesty, and it flies in the face of our lifesaving humility. Because humility gives us hope. It says in the *Twelve Steps and Twelve Traditions* that humility "amounts to a clear recognition of what and who we are, followed by a sincere attempt to become what we could be."

Many of us with mental disorders feel that we live in a kind of trap—that our illness completely defines "what and who we are" and places harsh limitations on "what we could be." Because our addictions have so violently exacerbated the symptoms of our mental disorders, we've come to believe that those disorders will always define us, wreak havoc in the lives we are trying to build, and drag us down into the muck of addiction over and over, no matter what we do. Our mental disorders have come to seem like the be-all and end-all of who we are.

But they are not. With sobriety, we begin to see that our symptoms can be managed. With honesty and humility, we begin to clearly see who we are, for better and worse, and this allows us finally to see all the possibilities for who we can become. It is the Fifth Step that opens this very practical door to Step Six, where we develop the true capacity for change.

Willingness

*Were entirely ready to have God remove
all these defects of character.*

OUR FOURTH AND FIFTH STEPS HAVE PLACED US in an entirely new relationship with ourselves, with others, and with what we identify as our Higher Power. We have found humility and honesty that we never imagined existed within us. And we feel as if we are, Step by Step, rejoining the world.

But our first encounter with the Sixth and Seventh Steps can be a little confounding. The last two Steps were clearly *action* Steps—there was something we could *do*. There are directions for how to do them in the Big Book and other Twelve Step literature, there are workbooks, there are workshops, there are suggestions, and it seems like every recovering person has a theory and a practical knowledge of how those Steps should be done. So we got down to it. We took our Fourth Step inventory; we sat down with someone and talked it out in our Fifth Step. We felt the whole vast range of emotions those Steps brought up in us—fear and trepidation, excitement and anticipation, and ultimately enormous self-discovery and real relief.

Then, having wrapped up Step Five, we opened the Big Book again, read three paragraphs, and found ourselves at the line, "We have now completed *Step Seven*."

What? What did I miss?

A whole lot. The Big Book isn't very wordy on Steps Six and Seven, and they are often overlooked. Many of us finish our Fifth Steps, and feeling the exhilaration of a newfound freedom from the secrets that had haunted us, get ready to roll and say, OK, what's next?

What's next, though, is something unexpected, and to many of us is pretty amorphous and unclear. Lacking practical direction, we're tempted to breeze through Steps Six and Seven in our hurry to get to more action—our amends list in Step Eight. But there's a great deal to these two Steps, and if we don't pay careful attention to what they ask of us, we miss out on some key preparations that make us ready for all the ones that follow.

And *readiness* is what Step Six is all about. We are becoming entirely ready to have our Higher Power, however we understand it, remove all our defects of character. This readiness to be relieved of these defects is what prepares us to do the hard work of the remaining Steps.

Isn't this a little vague? How do you become ready? What practical action does it entail? What do I do to get ready, and how do I know when I am? When I was on my first journey through these Steps, I got to Step Six and sat there absolutely baffled as to how this could be done.

So, in frustration, I turned to the Big Book and went back over those three paragraphs. I found that there actually *were* directions in there. Just after it finishes with Step Five, the book continues: "Carefully reading the first five proposals [Steps] we ask if we have omitted anything, for we are building an arch through which we shall walk a free man at last. Is our work solid so far? Are the stones properly in place?"

That's when I realized that Step Six is a place where I had the opportunity to pause, take a breath, and look back over how far I'd come. It was time to review the work I'd done, to make absolutely certain that I hadn't skimped on anything, hadn't avoided anything, hadn't told myself any of my old familiar lies or indulged in my usual self-delusions in an effort to make things easier for myself. I'd been working on developing a new level of honesty throughout my Step work so far. Now it was time to put that honesty to use in taking a real assessment of my sobriety at this stage.

For those of us with mental illness, Step Six is also a crucial opportunity to look at how far we've come in moving away from chaos and toward stability. This moment where we go back through the Steps, examining our work on each one, allows us to look at the changes we've made in our approach to our mental disorders as well. Here, too, we are becoming *entirely ready*, in this case to take on full acceptance and management of our mental illness. If we try to breeze through this Step, we're missing a stage of self-examination that's critically important to putting the knowledge we've gained about ourselves and our illnesses into practice. Here's our chance to see where we may not be entirely prepared, and to do that preparation right away.

This is a spiritual Step—not just because it includes the word God, but because it shows us just how far we have come and readies us to go yet further. At this point, we can look back at where we were when we started out and see the spiritual, emotional, and mental evolution that has occurred by working these Steps. Compare where you are now to where you were the day you faced that First Step, the day when you were crushed with the realization that you were truly powerless over your substance or addictive behavior. Look at that day, and look at all you've done—and all that the program, your Higher Power, and the people around you have helped you do.

In Step One, we did something we'd never done before: we faced the reality that we were beaten by our addictions. Even if we'd known for a long time that we were addicts, something changed when we *admitted powerlessness:* we stopped lying to ourselves. That moment of complete defeat was also the moment, surprisingly enough, where we began to have hope that things could change.

In Step One, those of us with mental illness also came to admit powerlessness over our mental disorders. We finally admitted to ourselves several things: that our lives were indeed unmanageable due to mental illness and addiction, that our addiction was making the unmanageability of our mental illness much worse, and that to continue to deny the need for responsible management would eliminate any hope of health or stability.

In this Step, we surrendered—not to the ravages of our addiction or our mental disorder, but to the truth of the fact that we'd tried to do it our way, and our way hadn't worked. It was time to try a new way.

So as we work Step Six, we review the concept of *surrender:* Have we *fully admitted powerlessness?* Do we harbor any doubts about whether we are addicts, whether we have mental illness, or whether those things will truly require ongoing management in our lives if we are to have real hope? If we do have doubts, now is our chance to examine them, discuss them with someone trustworthy, and finally let them go.

In Step Two, we *came to believe.* We came to believe that sanity, defined for us as management of mental health and freedom from addiction, was a possibility for us; and we came to believe that a Power greater than ourselves could restore us to that state of health and freedom. This step required that we give up our familiar notion that we could by force of self-will alone rid ourselves of our addictions or recover from our mental illnesses; it required that we recognize our own limitations and begin to believe in the power of something—whether that something was God, our Twelve Step group, our sponsor, our medication, our therapist, our friends and family—to help us find our sanity again. The point is that we came to believe in something larger than ourselves and were filled with the knowledge that we *would* find the sanity of management and recovery.

So for Step Two, we ask ourselves: Do I still, in the back of my mind, believe that self-will will do the trick? Am I laboring under the delusion that I can get well all by myself, or that I don't really need to try? Or, conversely, am I still convinced that there is no hope of ever finding health and peace of mind? Do I have doubts about whether sanity is a possibility for me? At this moment of reflection in Step Six, we examine our beliefs about sanity, hope, and a Higher Power. We look at the people all around us in our groups, see the clear evidence that recovery and stability are possible, and let go of our lingering doubts.

Having given up those doubts, we had the strength in Step Three to *make a decision.* It was a hard decision, the hardest many of us have ever had to make, and a decision we'll return to again and again: to turn our life and our will over to the care of our Higher Power as we understand it. In this step, we became *willing.* We recognized the truth that we are not running the whole show. We recognized that our best efforts had gotten us into this mess, and that if we became willing to turn our lives over to the care of something greater than ourselves, we would receive the guidance we needed to go in the right direction with our lives. Some began to trust God to guide them; others found that reliable guidance in their group, the Steps, their therapist, or their own moral center, making a daily commitment to do the next right thing.

As we contemplate our work on Step Three, we ask ourselves if we have fully *made that decision.* Are we holding back? Are we telling ourselves that we'll turn our will over sometimes but take it back at others? Are we trusting a Higher Power only in emergencies? Are we asking for unrealistic changes—like the removal of our mental illness, or freedom from having to manage it—and then getting angry when our demands aren't met? At this point in working Step Six, we get honest with ourselves about how completely we've let go of the notion that we are in charge. Instead, we take charge of what is truly in our control: the practice of recovering from our addiction and managing our mental illness. Here, we think hard about the Serenity Prayer, recognizing that true serenity does come when we balance letting go of what we can't control with taking responsibility for what we can.

Feeling the beginnings of serenity, we were further emboldened to move forward to Step Four. Here we ask this: Was I *fearless and thorough* in my inventory? Did I withhold information? Were there secrets I was trying to hide even from myself? Were there resentments I didn't list, or resentments I listed but am not yet willing to give up? What about with regard to my mental illness? Was I fully honest with myself about its effects on me and other people, the damage it's caused when I have not taken it seriously or treated it, or about the ways my addiction has worsened it? Did I allow the honesty of this step to show me how I need to change my behavior with regard to managing my mental illness? And, importantly, did I learn to differentiate between behaviors caused by symptoms and behaviors caused by addiction and character defects? These realizations are crucial as we work the Steps further. We need to know, on the one hand, when we are dealing with behaviors, thoughts, and feelings that arise from our mental illness, treating those effectively and without judgment; and, on the other hand, when we are dealing with behaviors and states of mind that arise from our addiction, treating those with increased efforts at working our program.

Having reviewed our level of honesty and thoroughness in our Fourth Step, we review our work in Step Five. First question: Did we do it? If not, time to get it done. Next: Did we do it with complete openness? Did we reveal the exact nature of our wrongs, or did we skim and hem and haw? Did we leave things out? Did we lie to God, to ourselves, or to that other person? How carefully did we turn the lamp on the dark corners of our past? Did we include the events and behaviors that arose from irresponsibility about our mental illness? Did we talk about hopelessness? And then, were we willing to take direction from the person we spoke to?

If we did all these things, we are doubtless feeling an enormous weight lifting off our shoulders. It is the weight of secrecy, self-hatred, shame, despair, anger, fear, resentment, remorse, and more—all of the things we have been carrying around with us for so long and that we are now letting go of, one by one. Step Six is a moment for spiritual revelation: *we have changed.* Many of us never thought we could. But we have. And we're only halfway through.

So here at the halfway point of our journey through the Steps, we take a deep breath, because this one requires that we dig even deeper into our stores of willingness and honesty. We have reviewed our work so far. And now we are well on our way to becoming *entirely ready* to have God remove all of our defects of character. But that means more effort and more change.

We used to fight change. I know I did. Change was threatening, even though I was always telling myself how badly I wanted things to be different—I wanted not to be drunk, I wanted not to be sick, I wanted things to slow down, be less chaotic, be different, be anything other than the way they were—and yet, curiously, I never seemed to be willing to do anything to change them. It's true that many people fear change and that we'll do a whole lot to stay stuck with what's familiar simply because we know it well. But addicts are particularly skittish about change, because it requires them to move out of their comfort zone, away from the self-destructive safety of their substance or behavior of choice. We may be in hell, but it's *our* hell, and many of us would rather stay there than risk the frightening world outside. And people with mental illness, in many cases, fear change because they fear things can never get better, only worse. So oftentimes, we cling to the known devastation and chaos rather than bother with what seems like a pointless effort to get things under control.

But we *have* changed. At this point in our recovery, we've changed a *lot*. When I got to Step Six and realized this was the case, I was stunned. I'd been convinced for as long as I could remember that I was stuck in my own private nightmare and that there was no way out—no way past the booze, no way past the mental illness, no way to live any kind of peaceful life, no way to reach anything like peace of mind. But when I found myself reviewing my work in the first five Steps, I found that I had become nearly unrecognizable—even to myself. And while that was really disorienting, it also meant that for the first time in my life, I was beginning to like who I was.

So, faced with the requirement of Step Six—*were entirely ready to have God remove all these defects of character*—I knew things were about to seriously change. And like a great many people embarking on this Step, I was scared.

This readiness means being totally open to a new way of life and a new kind of self. And going into it, you don't know what that life and self are going to look like. It's amazing how much we define ourselves by our defects of character. When I thought about my most glaring character flaws, they were these (and they were indeed glaring): anger and fear. Those weren't the only ones (not by a long shot), but they were big. And I was used to them. I still defined myself by them in many ways. So, I wondered, who would I be if they were removed? Who would I be if I weren't angry? Would I become weak? Get trampled by the world? And who would I be if I weren't, underneath all that bravado of anger, secretly terrified of everyone and everything? Part of me wanted these things gone, but part of me was so used to them that I was clinging to them with both fists.

But before we look at some examples of things that are commonly lifted from people in recovery, especially people with mental illness, we need to remind ourselves: *symptoms* of our mental illness are *not character defects*. So Step Six is not about asking for our *symptoms* to be removed. Our mental illness is part of our physical structure and isn't going to go away. We know it will probably get much, much easier to manage when we get the addictive substances out of our system and get our addictive behaviors under control, but we will still have genetic brain disorders that will sometimes act up. We will still have our bouts of depression, anxiety, mania, and other symptoms; it's important for us not to tell ourselves that we're "not working a good program" if symptoms set in. The trick here is accepting the presence of the brain disorder while doing all we can to manage it; meanwhile, we can work on the parts of our character, beliefs, and behaviors over which we have some control.

So how ready are we to have these character defects removed? We have to look at what we may still be hanging on to. These things serve us in some way, and figuring out how they serve us may take some close examination. Here are a few things I hung on to and that I know other people with mental illness sometimes hang on to as well:

- Envy. I was jealous of people who didn't have mental illness. I thought they had it easier than I did, didn't suffer as much, didn't struggle. For one thing, this just isn't true.

Everyone has struggles, everyone goes through suffering, and many people were struggling with far more than I ever had. For another thing, envy in my case was another word for "feeling sorry for myself." I had to get off my pity pot and learn something I was totally unfamiliar with, which is envy's opposite and its cure: *gratitude*. In asking for the defect of envy to be removed, I was not asking to be glad I had a mental illness; I was asking that my eyes be opened to all the other beautiful things in my life.

- Fear. I was afraid of my own shadow. Also of other people, going broke, failing, succeeding, doing laundry, saying the wrong thing, having symptoms, having serious episodes, losing the people I loved, dealing with my mental illness, not dealing with my mental illness, facing my addiction, not facing my addiction. But above all, I was afraid of myself. Like a lot of people with mental illness, I was scared of my mind and the way it worked and sometimes didn't work. I was scared of losing control, scared of the thoughts and impulses I sometimes had, scared of the confusion that sometimes overcame me, scared of the chaos that seemed to consume me, and scared of the chaos I seemed destined to create. But I was so used to my fear that it seemed to define me; I couldn't tell who I was apart from it. I couldn't imagine a life without it. When I became willing to have my fear removed, I also had to become willing to do what I could to make my own life less frightening, and that meant imagining a new life.

- Attachment to my disorders. Who wants to admit that they actually *like* some aspects of addiction and mental illness? Some of us are indeed attached, however ambivalently, to our disorders, and this is one of the reasons why: they are states of extremes, and they create extreme emotions in us. We get used to the thrills. We welcome them sometimes, and sometimes we even court them. We go off our meds; we do drugs that we know will exacerbate our highs; we drink to exacerbate both highs and lows; we get involved with people who feed into our illness; we don't keep up with our mental health appointments; we don't do the things that help keep our symptoms at bay; we rely too heavily on other people for things we could do ourselves, or blame things on our illness that are really our responsibility, and then we refuse help when we most need it; we do all sorts of things to destabilize our lives. And then, when we crash, we wonder what happened—and then we do it again. In recovery from addiction and mental illness, we need to be willing to let go of the thrill of extremes. That's hard, because we fear our life may be dull without them. But that just isn't what happens, as we soon learn. The rush of thrills is gradually replaced by the joy of peace of mind.

For me, those defects were just the tip of the iceberg. But you've got to start somewhere, so that's where I started in trying to let go of the familiar defects that caused me so many problems, but that I was so very attached to.

It's the rare person who can simply announce, "I'm ready!" all at once—I've never met one, and I have my doubts as to whether any exist. For the rest of us humans, readiness comes gradually, in fits and starts. Sometimes we're ready to let go of a defect one day and want to grab it back the next. In this case, we just keep letting it go again, every time we grab. This is a way of practicing patience with yourself, having a sense of humor about your humanity, and keeping some perspective on just how perfect you can be—which is not at all.

We have to bear in mind that in Step Six we are only becoming *ready*. No promises have been made to us about whether these character defects will be removed or when. I'm a pretty impatient person, and when I decided I was ready to have them removed, I wanted them all removed yesterday, if not sooner. Didn't happen. The important realization about Step Six is this: like the other Steps, it's not *just* a Step. It's not a quick glance over your work so far as you sprint toward the next six Steps. It's a permanent change in your approach to life. You're getting ready to become the person you will be.

The most important thing that this Step brings us is this: a vision for who we can become. Practicing this Step, we see that we have already changed, and we see that we're putting the discoveries of previous Steps to work. Surrender, willingness, honesty, humility, and acceptance are all at play as we recognize the truth of our addiction and our mental illnesses, as we face some truths about ourselves, and as we let go of the defects that are keeping us trapped.

There are so many places in the Steps where we are asked to take a flying leap of faith. So we look at the people in our groups who have what we want, and we see that *they* took those leaps. They worked these Steps; they became willing to be completely transformed, even though they didn't know who they'd be or what their lives would look like once that happened. Step Six is a big leap of faith. But we're ready for it. And so, having become entirely ready, we move on to a pretty profound turning point in the Steps: Step Seven, where the person we were begins to transform into the person we want to be.

Transformation

Humbly asked Him to remove our shortcomings.

SO WE COME TO STEP SEVEN *entirely ready,* and the Step wastes no time in putting us to work. Before we can begin this Step, we have to muster all the humility we can, because that's exactly what it takes to be transformed.

If it seems like the Steps are trying to bang the idea of humility into our heads, it's because they are. I know I for one was pretty hardheaded on this point. Humility was not something I was particularly familiar with, and even when I reached this point in my first trip through the Steps, I was still confused about the difference between humility and humiliation. Humiliation was a regular guest in my head. Humility was not. So when I reached Step Seven, I had to take another look at it. If I didn't, I had little hope of those shortcomings ever being removed.

What I found was that I'd been arrogant for a very long time. I had believed for years that I was going to fix all the ways I was broken by self-will alone. I'd convinced myself that one of these days, if I just *tried* hard enough, I was going to become someone different— someone better, someone I could respect, someone without all the glaring shortcomings I knew I had. I knew I wasn't the person I wanted to be. And I was clinging to the threadbare belief that I was capable of radical change on my own. I thought that not only could I change all the things I didn't like about my character, I could also work magic—I could put down the bottle without anyone's help, manage my mental illness without any effort, and overnight become someone new.

I couldn't. I'd tried everything—or so I thought—and I'd found myself at the same dead end. I was stuck there with the same self-hatred, self-doubt, and sense of absolute failure that I'd always felt. My combination of denial, arrogance, willfulness, and foxhole prayers hadn't worked. In other words, using my character defects to work on my character defects had failed miserably. I needed something else.

Here the Steps reminded me that what I was after wasn't just freedom from the bottle. I was after a whole new way of life. I wanted more for myself. And I wanted more *from* myself. Humility was the key.

Having worked Step Six to the best of my ability—having become as entirely ready to have my character defects removed as I was capable of at that time—I realized I'd already developed more humility than I'd ever had before. Humility is, in some ways, an acceptance of who we are and how we must live if we are to be at peace. I'd made some progress on that front. I'd accepted that my character flaws weren't going to go away on their own. I'd accepted that living in active addiction was not an option for me. I'd accepted the fact of my mental illness and the need to manage it responsibly. I was ready to change.

And I'd seen proof all around me in other recovering people that character defects could be removed and that a total transformation of character was possible when that happened. So I had a tentative faith that a change was possible for me, too. When I reached this Step, I was finally able to see that humility wasn't about humiliation—it was about hope.

At Step Seven, we are prepared to become new people. We are able to see, at last, that there is a true self underneath the grime of all the character deficits we've built up over the years—fear, anger, dishonesty, and all the rest of the things that kept us trapped in addiction, isolated us from others, and deprived us of any spiritual peace. That true self we are beginning to uncover is the one that can have those things that humility brings: sobriety, serenity, stability, usefulness to others, and the strength we need to meet any adversity life brings.

I had always wanted those things. But the total devastation of my self-respect brought on by years of addiction and untreated mental illness had convinced me that those things would never be possible. My vision for what I could expect out of life and what I could expect from myself was very grim. Like so many others, I had become convinced that the best I could hope for was simply to get by.

I had given up. And I was filled with the bitterness, resentment, and anger that come with a lack of hope. Where hope should have lived in me, I felt only despair—and it took me a very long time to understand how I had brought that despair on myself. It had become a character defect in its own right. I thought I had tried everything to create change in my life, but I had tried only running, fighting, and giving up. At Step Seven, we ask to be shown a new way.

This Step creates a lasting spiritual change in who we are. If we allow it to, it lifts us out of the hell of despair and shows us the people we can be and the things we can do. Before I got to Step Seven, I was still operating in great part on the force of desperation—I just didn't want to go back where I was. But when I honestly asked for my shortcomings to be removed, I began to see where I could go.

When we lack hope, we limit ourselves. We don't work on our character, because we don't believe it's worth the effort—we think that our character is flawed beyond repair and that we're destined to fail. Step Seven asks us to begin the work of character building. The first step in that is simply asking to be released from the character defects that have kept us trapped in our addiction and our unmanageability. When we are released from these, we find we have enormous room to move and grow. We're no longer stuck in survival mode. We can imagine greater possibilities for our lives and for what we can bring to the world.

When I was still using and still running from my mental illness, I was too busy trying to get what I wanted to work on who I was. I was completely stuck in my conviction that there was an easy way out of the life in which I was trapped: there was a quick fix for my alcoholism, there was a way to duck out of dealing with my mental illness, there was a way to get all the material stuff I wanted just because I wanted it, there was a way to outrun my past, my personality, and my pain. I spent so much time looking for these things that I had no room left over for thinking about what character traits I could develop that might get me out of myself and into the world. I thought I had nothing to offer, so I didn't bother trying.

The *Twelve Steps and Twelve Traditions* describes the situation so many of us have found ourselves in: when asked to choose "between character and comfort," most of us ditched character building in favor of our chase after happiness. Even though it seems very strange that I could have called the misery in which I was living any kind of "comfort," in fact it *was* comfortable—I was used to it, and it didn't require anything of me. I could live by instinct, seeking nothing but relief from pain. I never had to grow.

I couldn't see that my blind run away from reality and toward a fantasy of happiness was exactly what was causing that pain. And it was my lack of humility that was blinding me to the possibilities for real change. Blocked by the arrogant misperception that I could change by force of will, and disappointed again and again by the failure of my will to create change, I had been reduced to grabbing at whatever I could get my hands on that would get me through another day. My focus in life had narrowed to a single point: survival. And I couldn't grasp that my means of survival were killing me.

Survival, in those days, meant somehow keeping myself protected from the reality of my situation. So long as I could keep enough alcohol in my system, I could avoid facing my rampant mental illness, my deteriorating—and rapidly evaporating—relationships, my empty bank account, my disappointed family, my string of failures both personal and professional, and my own face in the mirror. So long as I could avoid these things, I could avoid the overwhelming task that needed to be done of cleaning up the mess and overhauling my life. I could avoid responsibility, and I could avoid growth.

Growth—character building, change, and the development of a moral center—requires a lot of work. And I didn't want to do it. What I was completely missing was the fact that it was taking just as much work, if not more, to avoid it. And the backbreaking effort to maintain this catastrophic level of denial and avoidance was sucking the life out of me. My devotion to this denial came at the expense of everything I said I valued: the people in my life, work, goals, dreams, and any sense of self-respect. My values had dwindled to include little beyond my own self-interest.

The *Twelve Steps and Twelve Traditions* hits the nail on the head. It talks about the fact that while many of our best efforts were well intentioned, still, "our crippling handicap had been our lack of humility." We were unable to see that strength of character and of our spiritual lives needed to come before material wealth.

I used to understand "material wealth" as simply stuff—money, property, that kind of thing. And while I was plenty greedy about those things, the material things I obsessively sought were more abstract: I wanted what everybody else had, or what I thought they had. I wanted their happiness, their confidence, their stability, the respect they got, the ease in their own skin that they seemed to have. I wanted their freedom from mental illness. I wanted their lives. I wanted their personalities. I wanted everything but what I had. And that kind of seeking—looking always outside myself, never within myself, for satisfaction and fulfillment—creates a gnawing spiritual hunger that can never be filled.

Addicts are painfully familiar with spiritual hunger. So are those of us with mental illness who cannot or will not make the choice to accept and manage our condition. In both cases, we are straining toward external sources of comfort, when the comfort we need can be found only in a rich and nourishing inner life.

When we live in addiction and unmanageability, our inner lives starve. We lose sight of who we are, what we value, and what we believe. We give up hope of creating stable, happy lives for ourselves and give up on becoming the kind of people we want to be. We live at barely subsistence level, and we are tangled in a net of resentment and hopeless resignation at our state. But if we work the first six Steps and become ready to have our defects of character removed, we can begin exploring who it is we are and who we want to become.

Many people find when they reach this point in their recovery that they have no idea whatsoever who they are. I was one of these people. I felt both overwhelmed by the idea of needing to figure it out and tentatively excited at the idea that there might actually *be* a core self in there, a self I might learn to rely on and respect. I had a sense that it was possible there was a purpose in my presence on the planet, something I'd doubted for a long time. And I had the hope that if I could free up all the space in myself that was being taken up by my character defects, I could use that space to develop character traits that reflected my values.

Those of us who by not taking care of ourselves allow our mental illness to go unchecked often suffer from the gradual erosion of our sense of self. Because of our own frustration and disappointment, combined with the stigma we live with and the internalized stigma we impose on ourselves, we can all too easily begin to see ourselves as little more than a collection of symptoms. We begin to define ourselves by our diagnoses. We sometimes feel that we *are* our chaos, *are* our episodes, *are* the moods or thoughts that we experience. It's vitally important as we go through recovery for us to notice all the ways in which we exist independently from our brain disease. We find as our illnesses become more manageable that while we still experience symptoms, we are beginning to know who we are *beyond* those symptoms. As we get to know our core selves, we begin to iden-tify our core values as well.

When I got sober, I saw myself as a walking state of chaos. I couldn't distinguish between myself and my bipolar disorder. I felt like I wore a sign on my forehead that said BROKEN. Because my illness was so out of control and so badly exacerbated by substance abuse, I didn't know what I was like when I wasn't sick—I'd been sick so long and so consistently that I had no state of stability to compare it to. So when I stopped drinking, started taking my meds, and started taking direction both in how I took care of my mental health and how I worked my recovery program, I found myself act-ing and thinking like someone I'd never met. It took quite a while for that state of stability to feel natural. It wasn't always comfortable at first, but it was a welcome relief from the mayhem of thoughts and moods that had tormented me for so long. Gradually, a *person* began to emerge from the constant state of illness and addiction. And that person was me.

It was humbling to finally acknowledge just how powerful my mental illness was, how powerful my addiction was, and how the two created an absolutely deadly combination. I realized I was damn lucky to be alive. This was lifesaving humility I was discovering. Finally understanding that my will was no match for the physical diseases that had consumed me, I developed a healthy respect for the force of mental illness and addiction. This respect took the form of acceptance. I accepted the fact that these diseases were a part of my genetic makeup and would require consistent and rigorous programs of mental wellness and recovery.

I also recognized that these things did not define me. They placed certain limits on choices I could make, and demanded a share of my care and attention, but they did not tell me who I was or who I could be. They didn't tell me what I valued or believed in, and they didn't tell me what I was capable of. But then, I asked my sponsor, what *did* tell me those things? How did I know, after nearly my whole life had been spent in unmanageability, illness, and addiction, what I valued, or what I believed?

"That," she said, "is the journey of recovery."

She was right. People in recovery who have found serenity are people who have given themselves over to the process of continuous *becoming.* And many people in recovery say they're grateful to be addicts, because it has brought them to a program where that process of becoming the people they're capable of being is encouraged and richly nourished.

At the Seventh Step, as we ask to be released from the trap of our shortcomings, we encounter an essential aspect of ourselves, the one that will get us through not only the rest of the Steps but through the rest of our lives: our spiritual core.

Many of us come to recovery with a sense of God, while others come with reservations about such a concept, and some have no faith in a Higher Power at all. But at this point in our work on the Steps, we've drawn upon some kind of spiritual strength more than once. Acceptance, surrender, willingness, honesty, and humility all call upon more inner resources than simply intellect can muster. So as we work Step Seven, whatever our spiritual beliefs may be, we are getting down to a deeper sense of our spiritual nature. We are recognizing that we already believe in—and have solid evidence of—the possibility of radical spiritual change, whether that change comes about through the workings of the Twelve Step program, a new reliance on the guidance of the people around us, our management of our mental, physical, and spiritual health, or our connection with a Higher Power.

Whatever path we take there, we have reached a new level of our spiritual natures. Whether or not we are believers in God, we can see that our willingness to accept guidance and assistance in our process of change has manifested nothing less than miracles. I never believed I could put the bottle down, but I did—because I stopped trying to do it alone. I never believed I could manage my mental illness, but I began to—because I started taking direction from the people who knew how it could be done.

Before, I'd tried to do everything my way, from bargaining with myself about how much I'd drink, to playing games with my medication, to keeping mental health appointments only when I felt like it, to sending up prayers for emergency assistance when things got bad enough. I never believed anyone else knew what they were talking about. I always thought the rules—especially the rules about medication and alcohol—didn't apply to me. I was always certain I could manage on my own. And it always had the same result: I made a complete mess of my life and health, and then, wow, did that make a believer of me—for a while. Till things got better. Then I'd stop taking my meds, start drinking again, go back to my old way of living, and the cycle would repeat.

Now, at Step Seven, I was ready to trust that there was a better way than mine. All the change that had already occurred as I worked the Steps wasn't something I could do on my own. So I knew it was something bigger than me that was going to do the rest of the changing. I knew that it was going to take spiritual effort and spiritual willingness on my part. And it wasn't going to be a onetime thing. Spirituality was going to have to become a permanent part of my daily operations.

This new perspective on who we are, on what we have to deal with in our lives, and on what we have to offer comes at an enormous cost. We have lost so much through our own rebellion against reality and have suffered deeply in our resistance to the truth of our characters, the nature of our mental disorders and addiction, and the guidance that could have saved us. Many of us have lost jobs, homes, financial security, and other material things; many more have lost loved ones and the relationships that provided us with support and a way of being connected to the world; and still more have lost self-respect, dignity, stability, and peace of mind. But these losses followed by the change in ourselves we have already seen in recovery stand as evidence to us that we can rebuild our lives, attain stability, and achieve serenity over time.

The *Twelve Steps and Twelve Traditions* talks about this cost and about what good it can bring with it. Reminding us to look around at our fellow recovering people, it points to the countless cases where we see devastation and unhappiness transformed by humility into new life and strength. It suggests we listen to the many stories around us wherein pain became a saving grace by bringing about a measure of humility, "which we soon discovered to be a healer of pain."

The pain we have felt at the hands of our addiction and our unmanageable mental illness has finally brought us to our knees. In recovery, we first feel healing as the symptoms of our addiction are relieved—the end of substance abuse and addictive behavior brings a measure of peace immediately. Soon, we feel the relief that comes when our mental illnesses are no longer being worsened by our addiction; our lives and mental health symptoms become more manageable, and we begin to see ways in which we can develop a consistent system of mental wellness and stability. Then, as the immediate crises of addictive behavior and uncontrolled mental illness are under better control, we begin to see that personality change other recovering people tell us will come. We start to uncover our healthy selves and our spiritual core. We begin to identify and act on values that are truly our own. Our moral center begins to develop and take hold. Healing, in so many ways, has begun.

Pain brought us to this place. But we are learning that pain is not the only motivator for growth. As I worked the Steps and saw the changes in my circumstances and mental health, I had practical proof that this way of living was going to keep me alive and was going to teach me to thrive. And as I felt the changes in my personality, values, and relationship with others, I had evidence of the necessity of ongoing spiritual growth. After years of subsisting on a life motivated only by a fear of pain, my reasons for living deepened to include much more.

My vision of what life could be broadened beyond the limitations I had set on myself. I began to see myself in connection with a larger world. I began to understand that not only could I participate in it, I had a responsibility to it as well. This connection with a larger world meant that I was no longer alone; this responsibility to that world meant that I needed to take care of myself so that I was most capable of contributing the things I had to offer.

"The Seventh Step is where we make the change in our attitude which permits us, with humility as our guide, to move *out from ourselves toward others and toward God*" (*Twelve Steps and Twelve Traditions;* emphasis added). We begin to see in working this Step that we must live in the world, not in the trap of our fear; we must participate and find sustenance in that world and contribute something to it as well.

And it is with this in mind that we say the Seventh Step Prayer. It doesn't matter what our conception of a Higher Power is; it doesn't matter if we even believe in one. All that matters is that we hear the spiritual message of this prayer and learn the lesson it has to teach us about who we can become.

> *My creator, I am now willing that you should have all of me, good and bad. I pray that you now remove from me every single defect of character that would stand in the way of my usefulness to you and my fellows. Grant me strength, as I go out from here, to do your bidding.*

We have begun the process of being transformed. Now, in Step Eight, we go on to transform our relationship with the world.

Responsibility

Made a list of all persons we had harmed,
and became willing to make amends to them all.

IN STEP SEVEN, WE TOOK AN ENORMOUS STEP out of ourselves and into the world. Step Eight now continues on our mission of becoming full and active participants in humanity. In this Step, we put the principles we've learned to practical use. As *The Little Red Book* tells us, members of Twelve Step programs "do not arrest alcoholism [or other addictions] or gain recovery by merely agreeing with the principles of AA philosophy—*they recover only if they live them.*"

Like a lot of people early in recovery, I thought Steps Eight and Nine were cruel and unusual punishment. I felt I'd done all the work I needed to do of facing my past in Steps Four and Five, by doing my inventory and sharing it with another person, and I had found it none too enjoyable. I couldn't for the life of me understand why, if I was on my way to a new life, I had to spend more time looking at my past—couldn't I just let it go? Forgive and forget and finally move on?

Not just yet. In truth, none of us can truly let go of the past until we have faced it and understood it, and that requires not just private consideration but action as well. Our past haunts us until we look at it squarely and allow it to teach us how to live—and how not to live—as we move on. When I got to Step Eight, I was in no mood to revisit my Fourth Step list—my resentments, grudges, fears, mistakes, and all the damage I had done—but I did hear loud and clear from other recovering people that this was not a Step I could afford to skip. If I did skip Steps Eight and Nine, I could look forward to yet more years rotting in my isolation, being eaten alive by my resentments, and, sooner or later, getting drunk and watching my mental illness spiral out of control once again. Instead of learning from the past, I would simply repeat it, as I'd done for so long. I'd repeat it till it killed me.

But if I worked these Steps *thoroughly*, if I looked at the past, took responsibility for my actions, and learned how to treat other people, then, people in recovery told me, I could find a place for myself in the world that I'd wanted to be a part of for so long.

The other night at a meeting, when someone was being particularly unhelpful to the group, a wise old-timer smiled and said, "AA is where we learn to play well with other children." AA is, for many of us, the first place where we have a chance to feel a part of something, to feel that we belong. And as such, it's the place where we get to practice participating responsibly in the larger world. The first step in that new, responsible way of interacting with others is going back and seeing what we can do about the damage to others we've already done.

The Big Book points out that this Step is not just about cleaning up our mess. That's only the beginning. "At the moment," it says, "we are trying to put our lives in order. But this is not an end in itself. Our real purpose is to fit ourselves to be of maximum service to God and the people about us."

We are in the process of becoming useful participants in the human community. For both addicts and people with mental illness, a real sense of one's own usefulness to the larger world can be painfully absent. By the time I sobered up, the havoc I'd wreaked on my own life and the lives of those around me had permanently damaged my ability to see myself as anything more than a waste of space. I saw myself as toxic, destined to create pain and suffering wherever I went. I wanted the opposite to be the case. I wanted to have something to offer to other people, and I wanted to be a useful person, but it seemed that between my alcoholism and my uncontrolled mental illness, I was nothing but a tornado ripping through people's lives.

Those of us with mental disorders are already carrying an enormous burden of shame, the weight of which can be literally crushing. This shame is only worsened when we do not take care of our illness, because our lack of manageability inevitably causes enormous damage to our lives and the lives of those who love us. When we don't take responsible care of our mental illness, we stand helplessly watching as it deals blow after blow to our lives, our relationships, our support systems, and our sense of worth. Substance abuse and other addictive behavior exacerbate the situation; soon, we can't tell if we're causing damage because we're addicts, or because we have mental illness, or—we often fear—because we're just hopelessly screwed up and can't ever change.

We can change, as we've already seen, by getting sober and working the Steps thus far. But we still may harbor a great deal of self-doubt. It's all fine and good that we can do all this work on ourselves, but do we really have the capacity to change the way we relate to the world? Many of us have very real fears of other people that are driven by our mental illness; many of us also understandably fear the ignorance and stigma that exist about our mental disorders. But those are things outside of our control. We can work to change them, but it won't happen overnight. Our project here is not to change the world; it is to take responsibility for ourselves and to change within.

That internal change does indeed open the door to a new kind of relationship with others and allows us a new kind of connection with the world.

Step Eight is the place where we take a practical step toward righting our wrongs. This Step has two parts. The first one looks relatively easy: we make a list. The second part looks a little harder: once again, we have to become willing to do something. Let's look at the list first.

We're making a list of all persons we have *harmed*. First question: What do we mean by harm? If we're like the average addict, we're bracing ourselves for a fight here—we're ready to go to the mat in our own defense over just about anything, insisting that we were not at fault and that we did not, in fact, cause harm. But we did. That's a fact. Whether through action or inaction, words or deeds, whether because we're addicts or because we didn't manage our mental illness, we have caused harm. The point of Step Eight is not to rub our faces in this. It's simply to assess where harm was done, so that it can be made right. So, the Big Book defines the word *harm* as something that causes "physical, mental, emotional, or spiritual damage to other people."

We usually don't need to look much further than our Fourth Step list to see a long line of people to whom we've caused damage on these fronts. The *Twelve Steps and Twelve Traditions* is not exaggerating when it says that in Step Eight we must make "an accurate and unsparing survey of the human wreckage" we have left in our wake. "Human wreckage" certainly described what I'd left behind. And an accurate and unsparing survey of it was necessary if I was going to undo some part of the damage done.

Where the Fourth Step was an exhaustive survey of our internal life in the past, the Eighth Step is an exhaustive survey of our life as it has affected other people. Our Fourth Step list gives us a good start on a list of those people. But because we have moved beyond Step Four and, in Steps Five through Seven, gained still more insight, honesty, and humility, we may well need to go back and fill in some gaps on that list. There are people we've forgotten about, things we did or said (or did not say or do) that our new level of honesty has brought to mind, and those people and acts need to go down on our list as well.

For those of us with mental disorders and addiction, Step Eight will include a process of taking careful stock of our past mistakes and clearly examining their sources. When we look at the people we have harmed and how we have harmed them, we need to determine which events and choices were driven by addiction and its character defects, and which were driven by mental illness and symptoms over which we may not have had control. If the harmful event or decision was indeed driven by mental illness, our next step is to determine whether it can be prevented in the future when we are taking responsible care of our illness.

When I was slipping quickly toward my bottoming-out point, I found myself in the grips of a profound depression. The depression was severe enough that I was unable to take care of myself, and so had been brought to live with my family. During this time, I was making some effort to manage my mental illness, or at the very least to get help climbing out of the hell I was in. One of the ways I was trying to manage it was to stay clean and sober, which I did succeed in for a short period of time. So while I felt awful for the extent to which I depended on my family, and wanted badly to be able to take control of my own life, and while they were in the painful position of witnessing my struggle, during this period I was not doing them harm. They may have felt burdened, but their help was given freely, and my needs were great through no fault of my own: my brain disease was ruling my mind and my life, and if I could have changed it, I would have.

But then I got drunk. And within days, I was causing a hell of a lot of harm.

That's where the distinction lies: was I capable of preventing that harm? Yes, I was. I could have stayed sober and continued my efforts to recover from the episode of mental illness that had me in its grip. It wouldn't have made dealing with my mental illness easy, but it would have prevented me from spinning yet further out of control. But I didn't stay sober, and suddenly all the problems my mental illness had created for me and my family were exponentially increased by the problems my addiction was creating. I went from nearly catatonic to explosively angry, unreliable, and dishonest. Soon, I slammed out of my family's house and went to live in a squalid apartment where I could drink myself to death without their efforts to help me stay alive and regain my mental health.

The harm I caused then was extensive, to my family members, to my relationships with them, and to myself. So when it came to making my Eighth Step list, I had to carefully examine that period of time to determine what damage I could have prevented, and what damage was an effect of a mental illness I could not control.

The key here is taking responsibility for the damage that is ours to re-pair. Both mental illness and addiction arise in us originally through factors we don't control. But the key difference between them is that with addiction we do have a choice: while we can't choose whether or not we are addicts, we can choose whether we *actively stay in addiction*. We can choose not to use substances and to stay in a recovery program. When we make the choice to continue to allow our addiction to rule us and wreak havoc wherever we go, we are causing harm that we will have to amend.

For some of us, it may be useful to draw up a separate list, one that includes people we have harmed primarily through our mental illness, whether by our failure to manage it or by the simple fact of it. It was helpful to me to have one list of people I'd harmed through addiction and character defects; those people I could prepare to make amends to by taking responsibility for my wrongs and by asking what I could do to make it right. For my second list, of people I had harmed through my mental illness, I had to honestly take stock of what behaviors I could have changed, what events I could have prevented, and what situations I could have handled differently, even though I had a mental illness. By the same token, I had to recognize that there were situations in my past that were the result of symptoms I could not have changed. For this list, I began to prepare to make amends for those things that *were* in my control. Looking over my past, I saw countless times I could have prevented harm done to others if I had been managing my mental illness. And then there were times when, despite my best efforts, symptoms emerged and caused harm to others, even though that was the last thing I wanted. For those events, I prepared to make amends by honestly explaining to the person I'd harmed that I had a mental illness, had not intended to harm them, and would do everything in my power not to let it happen again.

Making this separate list had a powerful effect: I recognized that I was less at the mercy of my mental disorder than I'd thought. Throughout the years of my drinking, I'd believed my mental illness had me by the throat and I was helpless to change its effects. In the process of working the Steps, I gradually gained both a healthy respect for the power of my mental illness and the need to manage it, and a healthy respect for my own capacity to direct my behavior and make my own choices most of the time. Knowing that I was not just a marionette being jerked around on strings by my mental illness gave me some badly needed confidence—and it gave me yet more proof that my mind and health were my responsibility. Taking responsibility for my mental health is the most practical, immediate step I can take in the project of participating in the world.

What kind of harm are we addicts prone to do? Among our more glaring defects are anger, dishonesty, and fear; the harm that comes out of these three things alone could fill volumes. We fight, we hide, we lie. We blame, we judge, we criticize. Other areas of likely harm come from other areas of defects: our desire for control leads us to manipulation; our fear of reality leads to denial; our avoidance of responsibility places a burden on others that we should shoulder ourselves; our desire for intimacy is mishandled and becomes either meaningless promiscuity or emotional dependence.

In all of these instances, we need to look carefully at whether we are dealing with symptoms of addiction and character defects or with symptoms of mental illness, which have nothing to do with character. The two often look alike. In Step Eight, we are careful to honestly examine each instance, always asking this question: *was this action driven by self-will or by my brain disorder?* In some instances, the answer will be clear; for example, unkind words said while I was drunk require an amend that acknowledges my addiction and character defects. In others, it will be a little cloudier; those same unkind words said when I was manic and not thinking clearly still require an amend, but this time when I make that amend, I will explain my mental illness and its effects on my behavior that I can't control. Under no circumstances do we blame our mental illness for actions over which we did have control.

And here's the kicker: for those of us with both addiction and mental illness, there are many instances when the symptoms of our mental illness were out of control *precisely because of our addiction* and in part because of our character defects. As we've seen again and again, we've done an enormous amount of damage simply by failing to

take care of ourselves. Much disaster could have been averted by
the choice to accept and manage our mental illness. And that is the
choice we are now making. In Step Eight, as we prepare to make our
amends, we are preparing to let people know that we have changed
in this way. Our "living amends" for harm caused by our unmanaged
mental illness in the past is our choice to manage it in the future.

As we make our list, we will likely be listening to a chattering mental
sound track of excuses, justifications, and endless reasons why harm
done was someone else's fault. This sound track is to be thoroughly
ignored. We are here to clean up our side of the street, not theirs; if
their side is messy, so be it. That is no problem of ours, and we can't
entertain feelings of superiority or justify our own wrongs because of
it. Our project is to take responsibility for our own stuff, and that's all.

One area of particular challenge in Step Eight for those of us with
mental illness may be a lurking sense that we *are* justified in some
of our faults. We may feel entitled to anger, especially of the self-
righteous variety. We may feel we deserve the occasional bout of self-
pity. We may enjoy a certain amount of resentment toward others,
whether toward people whose lives we assume are easier than ours,
or toward people who don't understand the very real challenges we
face. But anger, self-pity, resentment, and all the other defects of
character particular to the addict are not justified by the presence of
a mental illness. Much as I would like to think I'm entitled to feel all
these things, the reality is that when I indulge in them, *I cause harm.*
And then I wind up with yet another entry on my list of amends
to be made. Worse, when I indulge in them, I stay stuck in my old
ways of being, and I don't grow. I cut myself off from all the serenity
promised by a truly thorough working of the Steps.

When we stop judging and justifying, quit arguing and denying and
blaming, we are doing the second part of Step Eight: we're *becoming*

willing to make amends. We're getting pretty good at becoming willing to do things that we'd never have thought were possible before. In Step Three, we became willing to turn our lives and our will over to the care of a Higher Power as we understood it. In Step Four, we became willing to look honestly at ourselves, and then in Step Five we became willing to fully share what we saw with another person. At Step Six, we became willing to have some long-treasured character defects removed, and now, at Step Eight, we become willing to face our past and redress our wrongs in a very practical, literal sense. We're not just getting ready to sit down with an impartial third party to disclose our secrets. We're getting ready to face what many addicts fear more than anything: other people. And these are people we have some good reasons to fear. We've harmed them, and they're likely none too happy about it.

But if we can face ourselves—which many people never do—as well as a Higher Power and another person, we can certainly stand face-to-face with the people we've hurt in the past. By working the Steps, we've come to a measure of peace with ourselves. We're no longer running from the reality of ourselves or our lives; we know who we are, faults and all, and we are ready to change. This is one of the greatest gifts the program gives us. Similarly, accepting our mental disorders and deciding to manage them have brought us to a new peace of mind. Facing this challenge has given us a degree of acceptance and responsibility that many people never find. The suffering we went through to get to this point in our lives has ultimately brought enormous rewards. So becoming willing to make amends is really just a matter of drawing on the honesty, acceptance, and humility we've already developed.

To become ready, we need to continue to deepen our understanding of humility, because it is humility that allows us to forgive. Without the capacity for forgiveness, we will never be ready to make our amends. We have already seen how badly damaged we have been by our resentments—they act on us like rust, eroding our spiritual and mental health from within. The only cure for this condition is forgiveness, and the only means of reaching the capacity for forgiveness is humility. If I have the humility to understand that I myself am human, flawed, and innately imperfect, then I must understand that you are too; this humility makes it possible for me to forgive us both.

Humility and forgiveness shed a light on human nature that allows us to see ourselves and others more clearly. We are all "rightsized" in this light. It is human to fail, and human to strive to improve; as we see ourselves do both of these things, we have greater empathy for those all around us who are failing and striving as well. Humility and forgiveness release us from resentment, and we begin to see all we have in common with those people we once judged, resented, envied, and blamed. Finally we lose the sense that we are locked in a pitched battle with ourselves and the world as a whole. At the Eighth Step, as we prepare to make our amends, we let go of our merciless judgment of ourselves and everyone else, and gain new respect for the individuals we all are.

As addicts and people with mental illness, we have labored too long with a bitter sense of inadequacy and failure. The preparations we are making in this Step to bring ourselves into right relation with other people allow us to see that we are indeed equal to all others. Our mental illness does not make us less human or less worthy; it does not consign us to a private hell for life; the ways in which we have not fully realized our potential are no longer proof of failure but avenues of opportunity.

One of the most important areas of willingness we must develop in Step Eight is the willingness to forgive ourselves. It's self-destruction—

the harm done to ourselves—that we often forget when we are working our Eighth Step. "Few of us realize that our own names head the
list of those we have wronged, and that by living this program we
are first making amends to ourselves, to our outraged bodies, to our
confused minds, and to our troubled spirits," *The Little Red Book* says.
There is no question that we *have* been hurting ourselves; certainly
we have wreaked havoc on our bodies, minds, and spirits. Abuse of
substances and engagement in addictive behaviors have worsened
our brain disease and damaged our physical health in other ways,
and allowing the chaos of unmanaged mental illness to rule our lives
has eroded our spiritual wellness. As we work this Step, we need to
become willing to forgive ourselves as well.

Our relationships with others and with the world and our ability to
change those relationships depend upon that willingness to forgive
the harm we've done to ourselves. *The Little Red Book* notes that this
harm "may actually have given our emotions violent twists which
have since discolored our personalities and altered our lives for the
worse." For many of us, bitterness and anger have damaged our ability to relate to, care for, and interact with others. Our relationships
may have been baffling, painful, filled with conflict, and followed
by isolation; our whole idea of human nature and relationships has
become warped, and so has our vision of who other people are, who
we are, and how we may be a participant in humanity. For a long
time, we have carried our pain into our relationships and into the
world; in the Eighth Step, we are preparing to carry peace into these
things instead.

I think that the amend I needed to make to myself may have been
the one I was least willing to make. The years of chaos and damage done had so thoroughly destroyed my sense of self-respect that
I could barely stand to look in the mirror. My anger at myself was
enormous, far greater than my anger at anyone else. And despite my

knowledge that my mental illness was a brain disease I had not brought on myself, I had yet to really grasp that knowledge on an emotional level. Like so many of us do, I still carried the weight of internal stigma, and letting that go was a difficult task. We have been bombarded with the message that we are less worthy than other people, are hopeless, are personally responsible for our illness. When we then do cause harm through our own unwillingness to manage our illnesses, we take it as proof that we are innately damaged. This toxic combination makes for a great deal of shame, guilt, and anger at ourselves. This anger must be let go. We need to forgive ourselves, reject the stigma we face internally and externally, and believe in the possibility of change.

So as we make our Eighth Step list, we first identify the false beliefs and unhealthy personality traits that have caused harm to ourselves and to others. Being thorough as we examine our entire lives, we keep our focus on our own past, not on the actions of others. We ask where we were at fault; we forgive the wrongs done to us. We avoid extreme judgment both of ourselves and of others: the *Twelve Steps and Twelve Traditions* advises that "a quiet, steady view will be our steadfast aim."

And the *Twelve Steps and Twelve Traditions* goes on, telling us exactly what this Step is about: "It is the beginning of the end of isolation from our fellows and from God." Next, in Step Nine, we take action to break out of that isolated place, heal our relationships with others, and in doing so heal the damage we have done to ourselves.

Restitution

Made direct amends to such people wherever possible,
except when to do so would injure them or others.

WHEN I WAS ABOUT SIX MONTHS SOBER, I was immersed in Step Nine. It was a challenging, sometimes painful, truly inspiring process that was radically changing my life. I had made most of my easier amends, to acquaintances, colleagues, and people to whom I'd done definite but not crushing damage. I had opened the door to the long-term and permanent amends I'd need to make to my family. I had arranged for and started on my financial amends. I'd written letters to those people I could not meet with face-to-face, whether because they were no longer in my life or because they had told me flatly that they didn't want to hear it. And now I was faced with one big fat cleanup job I had been dreading and badly needed to take care of.

At the end of my drinking career, I'd left some very literal wreckage behind me. I'd spent two years in utter drunken insanity while living in California. By the end of those two years, I was psychotic, in and out of emergency rooms, psychiatric wards, and treatment facilities, and was not even fully conscious of what was going on around me, let alone capable of managing my own life. My family had come to collect me. It was an emergency situation—left to my own devices, I had stopped taking my meds, had drunk myself into repeated alcoholic crises, and had become suicidal—so they couldn't waste any time. I was put on a plane and taken to live at my mother's house. That meant I left my job, my house, my car, all my belongings, and my *cat* to the care of my understandably pissed-off friends. By the time I sobered up nearly a year later, I'd racked up such an enormous psychological and interpersonal debt I could hardly see where I would begin. But it was time to head back to California and see what I could do.

I cleaned up the logistical mess as best I could, collecting my things, taking care of arrangements, and making amends to the people who would still listen. Most of the people there wanted nothing to do with me. But my best friend had hung in there, more or less, and she and I went to dinner. There, I explained to her that I was (obviously) an alcoholic but was sober now, and was working the Steps. And I explained to her that I had finally started taking my mental illness seriously and was treating it every day—I was taking my meds, seeing my psychiatrist and therapist, and working my tail off to regain my mental health. I said I was sorry.

She was in no mood for apologies. She was chilly. She said, "Fine. So don't drink. And don't ever let your mental illness take over like that again. If you do, you'll be dead. And then you really *won't* be able to clean up the mess." She shook her head. "Don't tell me you're sorry," she said. "Just don't ever, ever, ever let it happen again."

That's what is meant by "living amends." We don't just *get* sober, we *live* sober. I'll talk more about living amends later in this chapter. But whatever type of amends we're discussing, this much is true: sobriety—and sanity—require that we take responsibility for our past, present, and future. They require that we take care of ourselves, physically, mentally, and spiritually, so that we are able to bring something valuable to others. And they allow us to participate fully in the world.

The work we do in Steps Eight and Nine transforms us. Step Nine is not, as it can seem at first glance, a punishment for mistakes we've made as a result of our addiction and unmanaged mental disorders. It isn't meant to make us suffer. It's actually spiritual work, meant to help us move beyond ourselves and into connection with the world. After years of the pain of isolation, this connection with the world is indeed transformative.

"Admitting and rectifying wrongs is a regenerative process necessary to our rehabilitation," it says in *The Little Red Book*. "It brings us spiritual understanding and develops spiritual strength that contribute to contented sobriety." Our "spiritual understanding" is deepened in Step Nine because it allows us a new, clearer view of human relationships, their power, and their potential as sources of spiritual sustenance. And the "spiritual strength" Step Nine brings is developed in our willing entrance into those human relationships, repairing those damaged, rebuilding those broken, and laying the groundwork for those that will come. A spiritual life cannot be fully realized when we are alienated from others; this Step brings us a new sense of spiritual connection with other people and with our understanding of a spiritual source.

With Step Nine, we become fully participating members of the human race. We take responsibility for our actions, become accountable to others, and learn to think beyond our own needs. We set right our wrongs and amend the harm we've done wherever we can. While this does not erase the past, it clears away the psychological, spiritual, and interpersonal wreckage we've left in our wake, so that we can begin to build new relationships on new terms.

Before we can do that, we must first clean up the damage we have done to others in our old lives. In Step Eight, we became entirely ready to make our amends. No one will tell you amends are easy.

But the Big Book reminds us that when we set out on our journey through the Steps, we said we would go to *any lengths necessary* to defeat our addiction, recover our sanity, and live a new life. Having made that commitment and having worked the first eight Steps to the best of our ability, we are ready to put principles into practice.

The principle at work in Step Nine is forgiveness. As we work this Step, we are not only asking others how we can be forgiven. In some cases, we are also forgiving them. And we are forgiving ourselves.

This practice of forgiveness allows us to let go of the last of the resentments that have been eating at us, and it allows us to let go of the anger at ourselves that has poisoned our relationships with others. For years, the fact that our unmanageability has caused such harm has created a toxic self-hatred. The guilt we've felt has tainted our ability to relate to other people and has made it nearly impossible for us to connect with the larger world. This in turn has created terrible isolation. We have developed the belief that our mental illness renders us incapable of forming healthy, lasting relationships. We have longed for emotional closeness but have watched ourselves destroy that closeness time after time, hurting others and bringing chaos into their lives.

For those of us with mental illness, Step Nine must be worked with special care. We need to be aware that we are not apologizing for brain disorders over which we have no control. Many of us carry a sense of guilt that we are sick in the first place; when we come to Step Nine, we may have a tendency to want to apologize for our illness itself. But what we are really trying to amend is the damage we've done that we *could* have prevented. Some of the harm we've done has been caused by refusing to manage our mental disorders; much of this has been through our active addiction, our use of substances, or our engagement in addictive behavior. We have triggered or worsened symptoms of our mental illness through our addiction, and this has caused harm for which we need to make amends. We have also, like every other addict, caused harm through character defects; we need to make amends for those as well. But we do not need to apologize for having a mental illness or for symptoms over which we did not have control.

Working Step Nine helps us to finally repair the broken ties, and it makes it possible for us to believe in our capacity for relationships in the future. It lifts the burden of guilt we have carried for so long. It frees us from the trap of our own past and moves us forward into a future where we are no longer alone. In this way, writes Kevin Griffin, our amends "transmute from a burden to a joy; from dreaded task to freeing leap; from drudgery to vital activity" (*One Breath at a Time: Buddhism and the Twelve Steps*).

The burden, at first, may seem very great. Those of us with mental illness sometimes feel we are looking back on an entire lifetime of damage, estrangement from others, social alienation, and shame. As we begin Step Nine, we may feel that we are taking on a task that is far from a "freeing leap"; instead, we may feel that it will drag us further downward into our own guilt and shame than we already are. But we're wrong. Working this Step, in addition to changing our relationship with others, changes our relationship with ourselves and with our mental illness. In facing our past, taking responsibility for our errors, and turning things around for ourselves, we gain a new vision of who we are and what we are capable of.

As I worked this Step and slowly began to lift the weight of my past, I started to see that I was not innately flawed, not inherently broken. I began to see that my mental illness did not make me a lesser person. I began to see that while I had *made* mistakes, I was not *myself* a mistake. It dawned on me that my mental disorder did not define me and that its symptoms did not consign me to a life of causing pain and chaos in my own and others' lives. As I began to repair my past, I realized that I no longer had to feel like a burden; I began to see that I had much to offer in relationships and that I could give love and support just as much as I needed them from others. I could finally see that I was not destined to cause harm; instead, I realized that freedom from addiction, management of my mental illness, and work on my character defects brought out all the gifts I had to offer the world.

In this way, it became clear to me that Step Nine was indeed about forgiveness. I was able to forgive myself, not only for harm I had done others, but for the damage I'd done to myself in carrying around so much self-hatred and shame.

When I came to Step Nine, I found myself wanting to apologize to everyone I'd ever met, for things I'd done or left undone, for things over which I had control and things I did not, for damage created by my addiction and damage I thought I'd done through my very existence. I wanted to apologize for *myself.* But I didn't need to do that. That desire came from a deep sense of shame about the fact that I have a brain disorder, and that shame was something that I had to let go. So as we work Step Nine, we need to carefully determine where we are responsible for harm done and where we are really seeing symptoms.

When I reached Step Nine, I had to make a distinction. Looking at each person on my amends list and looking at the particular harm done, I asked myself: Was this situation caused by alcohol, drug abuse, and the character defects at their core? Or was it caused solely by organic brain disease? In almost every case, I found examples of both. I looked at the damage I'd done to my family; there were situations where I'd created fear, resentment, anger, and grief by engaging in my addiction and by not managing my mental disorder, and there were also situations where those same things had been caused by symptoms of my mental disorder that I could not have controlled.

How do we approach this confusing situation? With deliberation, self-awareness, and honesty. Under no circumstances could I blame certain instances of, for example, manic impulsivity *that I could have prevented* on the fact that I have a mental illness. That was just shirking responsibility as I'd done for so long and in so many ways, and refusing that responsibility would neither help me nor heal my damaged relationships. By the same token, under no circumstances should I blame myself for manic episodes *organic to my brain disease.* That would only deepen my unhealthy sense of shame and would exacerbate misunderstandings between myself and the people around me.

How could I tell the difference? In most cases, truly, it wasn't that hard: if alcohol or drugs were involved, I was responsible. If the action came about during a period when I wasn't making an honest and significant effort to manage my mental illness, I needed to own up to that as well. If the act was entirely based in character defects—as opposed to symptoms—things like selfishness, dishonesty, denial, or resentment, then that was damage for which I needed to take responsibility.

Most of us know our character defects all too well, and if we are honest, we *can* tell when they're running the show. There were some harder calls—for example, determining when my alcoholic rage had caused damage, as opposed to when anger was appearing as a symptom of my mental illness. In those cases, I needed to get as honest with myself as I possibly could, look at whether I had been using drugs or alcohol or engaging in addictive behaviors at that time, and acknowledge whether I'd been making every effort to manage my mental illness.

When in doubt, I expressed that very doubt to the person to whom I was making amends. I first acknowledged that I'd done harm, then explained that I had been suffering from both addiction and mental illness at the time, and told them honestly that I didn't know which disorder had caused the event. Ultimately, I expressed sincere regret and explained to them that I was now actively working on my recovery from both addiction and mental illness. And as in all cases where we make amends, I asked what I could do to make it right.

"Making it right" can take many forms. We have already begun to make things right by stopping our addictive behavior. Our second action in righting our wrongs is our work through the Steps. People have called the Twelve Steps "an amends in Twelve parts." So when we approach people in making specific amends, we can begin by making it clear that the immediate cause of our damaging actions—our addiction—has been arrested. In many cases, this will also involve explaining that our mental illness was exacerbated by our addictive behavior and will no longer be allowed to run rampant in our lives. We can also explain the work we're doing in the Steps and help the person understand why this work is not only mitigating the immediate source of our chaos but creating lasting change in our behavior as well.

In some cases, people will not know much about mental illness, and we may have to give some explanation of ours, its symptoms, and how it may have contributed to any harm we have caused. From there, "making things right" will depend upon the person or institution we have harmed.

Still, Step Nine can be understandably intimidating. I've known a lot of people who've earnestly worked their way right up through Step Eight, and then, telling themselves that the people to whom they needed to make amends would reject their efforts, jumped straight ahead to Step Ten, on the theory that taking responsibility *from here on out* would be good enough. Not quite so. Step Nine needs to be done, honestly, thoroughly, and without delay. I've seen too many cases where Step Nine was skipped or put off indefinitely and the person wound up back in their addiction.

However, it's essential to remember that if we fear that our mental health will be destabilized by a Ninth Step encounter, that encounter should wait. Being discerning and honest with ourselves about our readiness for each amend reflects the fact that we are taking care of our sanity. Amends should not be made when our mental illness is actively causing trouble in our daily lives. That just isn't the time. Episodes of depression, mania, paranoia, anxiety, obsession, or other symptoms will interfere with our clarity of thought and intent. It's necessary to wait until the episode has stabilized and we are as symptom free as possible again.

But truly, if it is only fear for our ego that stops us, that just isn't reason enough. "Self-centered fear," as we've seen already, has been the cause of some of our worst mistakes and is the source of much of our isolation. We can't allow it to steal away the healing Step Nine offers to us and to others. For this Step, we need courage. We may think we don't have the guts to follow through, one by one, with the amends we need to make, but looking back over all the fear we have conquered already by working these Steps, we see plainly that our courage is much greater than we thought. Now we need to put it to use. If we don't, we're dead.

Our amends list may fall into several categories. Most of us have done the worst harm to our families, whether our families of origin, our own partners and children, or—in most cases—both. Many of us have also done considerable damage to friends and other support people, and many may have amends to make to business associates and employers as well. There may well be financial amends that need to be made, whether to people who've loaned us money or to financial institutions. In some cases, there will be amends to be made if we have committed crimes. And we should also list those amends that cannot be made without causing harm to another person. It's helpful to divide our list of people according to which group they fall under: Family, Friends, Other Support, Business/Employment, Financial, Criminal, and so on.

Then we figure out how we are going to approach each person on each list. This brings us to the point where we need to determine which *type* of amend is appropriate. The *Twelve Steps and Twelve Traditions* advises that the qualities we need right now are "good judgment, a careful sense of timing, courage, and prudence." And the Big Book reminds us, "There is a long period of reconstruction ahead . . . A remorseful mumbling that we are sorry won't fit the bill at all." With those things in mind, we can begin.

There are those amends that can be made immediately—people we should seek out ASAP. Pick up the ten-ton phone and make that call: ask to meet in person, lay out your situation and the work you are trying to do, and ask how you can make the situation right. Your goal is to repair the breach as best you can by taking responsibility for your actions. It's entirely possible this person may reject your advances out of hand. I've been told more than once to go to hell. That's not the point. The point is to *do our part*. If rejected, you can hope that sobriety, mental health management, and their effects on your future behavior will restore the relationship. That may happen, and it may not. Simply take responsibility, and let expectations go.

Then there are those amends where action should wait. This is often the case if the harmful situation is fairly recent and the relationship is still smarting from it. It is also often the case with family members or friends who have heard you say you're sorry more times than they can count, and they just don't buy it anymore. It took a long time for all the damage to compile, and it may take a long time to sweep up the mess. In these cases, make a beginning.

Once these friends and family members are aware that you are sober, working the Steps, and actively managing your mental illness, let the individuals know that you would like to have a discussion with them, when they're ready, about the past and the harm you've caused. In some cases, these people may be willing to read the Big Book, a book on your mental illness, or other literature that you feel will help them understand your conditions. If they're willing to do this, it may help them recognize the seriousness of what you're trying to do, and be more open to the idea that you're really working to change.

There are likely also family members and friends with whom there has been a serious and possibly irrevocable break. Divorces or separations, estranged parents or other family, lost children, close friends who have been alienated—amends must still be made to these people, but it may take some doing. Whenever possible, reach out to these people, whether by letter, phone, or through a third party. Let them know that you are sober and managing your mental illness, and tell them that should they ever be willing to hear from you, you would like the opportunity to make amends. Then allow them to come to you.

In the meantime, many sponsors recommend that you make some "creative amends" immediately. Write these people a letter you don't plan to send, or sit down with your sponsor and say all the things you would say to them if they were right there. Again, limit this to taking responsibility for harm you've done, detailing your understanding of the ways in which your addiction and unmanaged mental illness caused damage and asking how you can right the wrong. These people may never actually hear your amend. But it must be made, to the best of your ability, in good faith. Just because you cannot immediately reach these people does not mean you should not take action *for your own sake*. Amends are meant to heal both parties; do not skip these difficult ones just because circumstances are not conducive to a face-to-face meeting.

Financial amends, while sometimes painful, are fairly straightforward. Go to the person or institution to whom (or to which) you owe money, tell them of your situation, and offer to start repayment immediately. If your financial situation is limited—most of ours are, in early sobriety especially—then be honest about what you can afford. Offer to make that payment on a regular basis until the debt is repaid in full.

Finally, there are amends we cannot or should not make or can make only in part, because of the line in Step Nine that reads *"except when to do so would injure them or others."* First of all, be honest with yourself. Are you really afraid of doing the other person harm, or are you avoiding an amend you could actually make? If it's the former, then don't go crashing into an amend that will only cause more harm. Discuss the circumstances about which you're unsure with a sponsor, a trusted friend, your therapist or psychiatrist, or a spiritual person who can give you guidance. Listen to their advice, consult your own conscience and best judgment, but remember the point made in the *Twelve Steps and Twelve Traditions:* "we cannot buy our peace of mind at the expense of others." Our peace of mind, in these cases, may again have to come via creative amends.

As we work our way through our list, we'll run into some of our old demons. First we'll hit our natural defense mechanisms: we'll insist that the person we have harmed was just as much to blame, if not more so, for the conflict or the harm done. In this area, we need to remember that we are not the only ones around here who have emotional shortcomings and problematic qualities; other people do as well, and that is not our concern. Besides, we can come up with countless cases where it was our behavior that exacerbated any shortcomings they might have had. Here the important thing is just to redirect our attention to our part, and *only* our part. Blaming them will not heal us or heal our relationship with them.

We may also run into a great big roadblock of overblown ego. We are about to come face-to-face with people whose opinion of us may be pretty low, and rightly so; these are people who have reason to be angry and hurt and who may see us in a decidedly negative light. It's not surprising that these are exactly the people we'd like to avoid, preferably for the rest of our lives; even imagining the look on their faces when we see them stops us dead in our tracks. It would be very convenient if we could keep the scariest ones off the list. But we can't. Those people deserve our best effort to make amends, and we often owe them a great deal. Here we have to dig deep into willingness, because it won't be easy on our ego—but it will be healing for our character, our relationships, and our soul.

And here's a point of resistance I took up like a battle cry: *But I was only hurting myself!* Many, if not most, addicts suffer from this delusion. They think their drinking or addictive behavior goes unnoticed by others; they think that it doesn't interfere with their relationships, or work life, or financial well-being, or really anything at all. We can convince ourselves that only we are suffering. And plenty of people with mental illness insist that our refusal to manage our disorders causes no one else any harm.

On both fronts, we're wrong. In one way or another, our mismanagement of our lives, our chaos, our unmanageability, our character defects running rampant, our repeated crises all take their toll on the people in our lives. I managed to persuade myself that my drinking and denial of my mental illness were only hurting me. That, as the *Twelve Steps and Twelve Traditions* notes, "is the end result of purposeful forgetting." I expect that my ravaged family, scared and overburdened friends, confused and put-upon colleagues, and all the other people who were getting trampled by my addiction and untreated mental illness would have been very surprised to learn that I was "only hurting myself." In a literal sense, yes: I was pickling only my own liver and destroying my own brain. But we live within a human web, affecting each other profoundly every day. We need things from each other and offer things as well. When one part of the web is self-destructing, as I was, it is destroying the whole.

Some of the people we will be approaching with the intention of making amends will indeed have done us harm. And some of that harm has struck directly at the heart of what we are now trying to heal: there are many instances when our mental disorders have been misunderstood, discriminated against, and deeply stigmatized by people who did not know anything about the nature of mental illness. These people have sometimes been close to us, and their failure to understand has been the most painful and often damaging. Sometimes it has been institutions that have failed us, and that has created enormous anger and resentment in us. But if there are ways in which we have failed them as well, however understandable our desire to lash out has been, and however natural our anger and hurt, we still need to find a way to make amends.

These amends, when these people are no longer a part of our lives or still don't understand what mental illness is about, or when institutions are simply inaccessible to us, may be little more than our active forgiveness. Letting go of that resentment through forgiveness not only lightens our load, it actually changes our entire relationship with the world. We begin to see people with the compassion we would want them to afford us, and we begin to have that compassion for ourselves. We begin to understand the meaning of "live and let live."

And these are areas, too, where "living amends"—our efforts to re-cover from addiction and manage our mental illness—may be just as important.

"If life is a story," writes Kevin Griffin, "then living amends moves the narrative toward growth and healing and away from destruction and pain" (*One Breath at a Time: Buddhism and the Twelve Steps*). That friendship I mentioned at the beginning of this chapter and many others have been repaired. I am grateful for these friendships, which have flourished as the years have gone by and I have steadily grown in sobriety, serenity, and sanity. These things form the foundation of the kinds of relationships we have always wanted but that have so often eluded us or been grasped briefly only to be broken off by our illnesses. Those relationships are one of the gifts of Step Nine—they are the web of human closeness, of giving and receiving, of living healthy, spiritually sustaining, interconnected lives.

Now, having cleared away the wreckage of our pasts, we are ready to learn how to live in community, in sobriety and sanity, as we go forward into a new day. In Step Ten, we learn how to ensure that we keep ourselves mindful, in that day, of all we need to do to maintain sobriety and growth.

Commitment

*Continued to take personal inventory
and when we were wrong promptly admitted it.*

HAVING COMPLETED STEP NINE, we have rejoined the world of the living. Our past no longer needs to haunt us; we have faced it honestly, faced the people we have harmed, and recognized the ways we have harmed ourselves. This willingness to finally deal with where we've been has prepared us for where we will go now. This is the Step that teaches us how to maintain the sanity we have developed, and how to do so in a way that benefits not only us but also the world we live in.

At this point in the Steps, we need to recognize that we have done an enormous amount of work and have witnessed in ourselves and our lives the kind of change we'd never have thought possible. But this change is only the beginning. We've now reached what are often called the "maintenance Steps." In the next three Steps, we put the changes we've made into daily practice. Here, the Big Book offers a few words for us on our future in sobriety, serenity, and sanity. The following passage, often referred to as "the Promises," goes like this:

> If we are painstaking about this phase of our development, we
> will be amazed before we are half way through. We are going
> to know a new freedom and a new happiness. We will not regret
> the past nor wish to shut the door on it. We will comprehend

117

the word serenity and we will know peace. No matter how far down the scale we have gone, we will see how our experience can benefit others. That feeling of uselessness and self-pity will disappear. We will lose interest in selfish things and gain interest in our fellows. Self-seeking will slip away. Our whole attitude and outlook upon life will change. Fear of people and of economic insecurity will leave us. We will intuitively know how to handle situations which used to baffle us. We will suddenly realize that God is doing for us what we could not do for ourselves.

Are these extravagant promises? We think not. They are being fulfilled among us—sometimes quickly, sometimes slowly. They will always materialize if we work for them.

The Promises are read at the opening or close of many Twelve Step meetings. When I heard them early in sobriety, I thought they were nonsense. It was inconceivable to me that I would ever understand, at any deep level, the word serenity; I had no hope that I would ever get to a point where I did not regret the past; it was impossible that my experience could benefit others and more unlikely still that my feeling of uselessness would ever disappear. The notion that my fear of people would leave me was unimaginable. The idea that I would know how to handle any of the situations that still baffled me—which amounted to *most* situations—seemed unlikely in the extreme.

The only part of the Promises that actually clicked for me at that point was this: "They are being fulfilled among us—sometimes quickly, sometimes slowly." It was true. Everywhere around me, I saw these promises coming true in the lives of other recovering people. I saw people laughing. I saw them losing the fear that had haunted them. I saw them becoming useful, more focused on others, more confident in their capacity to help. And I saw that their "whole attitude and outlook upon life" was changing day by day.

And then, with time, with dedicated work on the Steps, and with commitment to maintaining my mental health, the Promises began to come true for me.

It was, in fact, as I embarked upon Step Ten that I began to realize this was the case. One day in my regular meeting, the person who was supposed to tell their story didn't show. The group leader said, "Would someone else like to step in and tell theirs instead?" And before I knew what I was doing, I piped up, "Sure!"

This isn't, on the face of it, such a big deal, unless you know that I'd been sitting in meetings every day for months and months and months and hadn't yet managed to say more than my name. I'd been tied in a knot in my folding chair, passing every time it was my turn, and bolting whenever anyone tried to so much as say hello. So when I announced that I'd tell my story, the whole group pretty much fell out of their chairs all at once.

It was a "situation which used to baffle" me that suddenly I knew "intuitively" how to handle. It was a moment when I realized that my experience really *could* benefit others. I felt like something needed to get done, and I could be of use by doing it. "That feeling of uselessness and self-pity" suddenly slipped away, and I told my story because someone needed to tell a story and mine would work as well as any. And while the group was shocked to learn that I could, in fact, talk, they weren't half as shocked as I. They had no way of knowing what I knew, which was that the Promises were coming true in my life at that very moment, in however small a way.

Step Ten is really very simple. The Big Book tells us that what we have to do is watch for character defects, immediately ask for them to be removed, discuss them with another person, and make amends if necessary. Then, it says, we "resolutely turn our thoughts to someone we can help." This takes us out of ourselves and puts us to use. But for all its simplicity, Step Ten offers us a myriad of benefits, spiritual, mental, and emotional; and for those of us with mental illness, it also serves to keep our health on track.

Step Ten appears at first glance to be just a practical matter, and in a way it is: we take inventory, a simple practical action. But really the Step is about spiritual growth. By the time we reach Step Ten, we have discovered a quality of spiritual awareness that was never accessible to us when our mental illness and addiction were ruling our lives. In those years, chaos and unmanageability, pain and isolation, shame and regret colored everything we saw. But the principles we have been practicing as we've worked the Steps have allowed us to tap into a spiritual place in ourselves, a place of peace and clarity. That clarity is a far cry from the fog of confusion in which we lived for so long. We no longer try to live by fumbling and swinging blind; instead, we can see clearly what our next Steps on the lifelong journey of recovery must be.

We've been told before that the Steps are meant to be worked, re-worked, and put into practice in our daily lives. In Step Ten, by continuing to take personal inventory, we practice—every single day—using the qualities of honesty, humility, and willingness that we've developed in previous Steps. On a very practical level, we see where our character defects are cropping up, where we cause harm, and where we need to make amends; and we keep a close eye on the status of our mental health. Taking personal inventory is that lifetime practice of keeping our side of the street clean, keeping our health intact, and keeping ourselves on track mentally, spiritually, and emo-tionally. It's how we maintain stability, and how we continue to grow.

The inventory is also how we stay in today. Addicts and people with mental illness have developed a habit of dwelling in the past and leaping forward into a fantasy of the future; rarely are we half as skilled at living in today. This is a direct cause of many of the messes we've made and much of the pain we've experienced. Our sobriety and our sanity depend upon the development of an ability to stay present in our lives, in this moment, right here, right now. *Here* is where we meet our responsibilities, sustain our relationships, and manage our mental health. *Now* is when we make choices and take action to maintain our sanity and our sobriety.

The Big Book says, "What we really have is a daily reprieve contingent on the maintenance of our spiritual condition." For those of us with mental illness, that daily reprieve is also based on the maintenance of our physical well-being. If I stop taking care of my spiritual life, I get drunk, and then I get sick. If I stop taking care of my mental health, I get sick, and then I get drunk. I have to take care of these things *today*—here and now. Not tomorrow. Not later. I have a one-day reprieve. I work this program one day at a time.

Mental illness and addiction are lifelong challenges that we face. They are not cured now, and they won't be cured later. Our continued recovery from them, our sanity and our sobriety, depend upon daily effort. We don't work the Twelve Steps and say, OK, I'm sober now! And we don't take our meds for six weeks and say, OK, I'm all better! We might wish it worked that way. But it doesn't. And in fact, recovery as a *lifelong practice* teaches us far more and helps us develop into better people than a quick-fix miracle cure ever could.

So it is that a daily inventory comes into play. Developing this practice is part of our "daily reprieve" from addiction and instability. You've probably heard by now the old adage that while you're staying sober, your addiction is doing push-ups in the other room, keeping itself in shape to take over your life again if you open the door. The same holds true for mental illness. Mental disorders are progressive by nature; we can arrest their progression by taking care of ourselves, but if we let up on that practice of self-care, the familiar instability and sickness will return in force. So doing a daily inventory of the ways we are maintaining mental, emotional, and spiritual health, identifying areas where we have fallen short or need improvement, and taking pride in areas where we are making progress keep us mindful of just where we stand in relation to sobriety and mental wellness.

This practice prevents not only a return to addictive behavior but also what they call "dry drunks"—you're not drinking or using, but you're also not spiritually or emotionally healthy, and you're not making progress. A daily inventory keeps you progressing. If you're taking stock honestly and thoroughly every day, you're less likely to allow resentments to build up, anger to fester, guilt to develop, relationships to deteriorate, and spiritual fitness to fall apart. In short, your character defects are kept in check. You are able to move freely through the world unencumbered by them, seeing damage where it's done and correcting it as quickly as you can.

And an inventory helps us prevent slips in our mental health care. If you're keeping track of symptoms as they happen, staying on top of all your treatment methods, and being open and honest with the people in your support system, it's less likely that an episode of illness will crop up, and when it does, you'll see it coming much sooner than you used to. This allows you to get as much help as you need as soon as you need it, and that makes it possible to prevent the kind of damage to you and the people around you that your mental illness did when it wasn't managed well.

In my life before sobriety and mental health management, I could go from emotional and mental stability to total insanity in seconds flat— or at least it seemed that way. One minute my relationships would be healthy, I would be pretty happy, work would be going well, my daily life would be running smoothly; and the next minute, without warning, my relationships were collapsing, I was an emotional and mental wreck, work was falling apart, and every area of my life was spinning into chaos. In truth, that's not how it worked. What really happened was that I was rarely honest with myself about how I was doing, and I never kept any kind of track of my mental or emotional health. When resentments came up, I stuffed them. When I was angry, I let it fester. When I was sad, I swallowed it. When symptoms of my mental illness started to flare, I tried to hide them from others and did my best to ignore them myself. All of this ignoring, denying, stuffing, festering, and swallowing turned me into a ticking bomb. Eventually, of course, I'd go off. And my life would blow apart all over again.

A daily inventory makes this kind of situation close to impossible. Being honest with myself every day forces me to face emotional distress, deal with it, and move on; it requires me to address character defects that are cropping up before they take over my behavior and relationships; and it ensures that I know right where I am in terms of my mental health and quickly register everything from mood swings to missed meds.

And by keeping me honest with myself, Step Ten also keeps me "right-sized." Maintaining a clear-eyed view of who I am and how I'm doing, I'm less likely to get cocky, with regard to either my addiction or my mental disorder. Addiction is, as the literature always says, "a subtle foe," and mental illness doesn't always send a formal announcement that it's coming. I have to maintain a healthy respect for the power of both and keep an eye on my areas of vulnerability to them. My greatest vulnerability lies in my own illusion that I have them beat. If I ever believe I'm finally "well," I can rest assured that I'll get knocked on my butt pretty soon. Step Ten helps me remember that my strength, sobriety, and sanity come from honesty, humility, and acceptance.

Acceptance is key to working Step Ten. In its words about this Step, the Big Book says, "We have ceased fighting anything or anyone . . .

For by this time sanity will have returned." This is a line that goes through my head every day as I work this Step. When I find myself fighting other people, or fighting the reality of my mental illness, or fighting the fact that I am an addict, I bring myself up short and think of these words. Fighting breeds resentment, denial, and anger, and for me these things are deadly. They are character defects that have brought me to my knees before and gladly will again if I let them. When I stop fighting, though, denial falls away, resentments are lifted, anger is relieved, and acceptance enters in. And when I have acceptance, I have willingness. I become willing to do the next right thing, willing to take responsibility, willing to live and let live, and willing to take care of myself. These things are all necessary to the "maintenance of my spiritual condition," the maintenance of my mental health, and the maintenance of my sanity.

This maintenance is the day-to-day action we take as part of a lifetime process of ongoing recovery. Every day, we take action to stay sober and grow in sobriety, and we take action to regain our mental health and manage it well. Our actions in the Twelve Step program include going to regular meetings, working the Steps, meeting with our sponsors, and doing service work (we'll get to more about service work in Step Twelve). Our actions on behalf of our mental health include some combination of taking our medications, meeting with our professional support team, getting enough sleep, exercise, and nutrition, developing life skills, and attending to other components of a thorough mental health care program.

Staying sober and optimizing mental health are not passive matters— they require a lot of effort. While we may not always want to make that effort, it always pays off, and not following through always burns us. If we resist daily maintenance of any aspect of our spiritual, mental, or emotional health, all the other aspects suffer. If spiritual health is neglected, mental health deteriorates; if mental health is neglected, spiritual health falters. If I'm not actively working on my sobriety, my sanity slips, and if I'm not actively taking care of my sanity, my sobriety is at risk.

We are whole people composed of many interdependent parts. When we were still in active addiction and our mental illness was still unmanaged, we felt like we were fractured, broken, always struggling to hold mind and body together, and failing at the attempt. Stability and sanity come with our active efforts to integrate who we are, to care for ourselves as human beings with mental, emotional, and spiritual lives that make up intact, healthy people. Step Ten is an essential piece of the puzzle. Taking daily inventory keeps us integrated, mindful, responsible, and aware.

It also helps us integrate past, present, and future. The Steps we've already worked have helped us face and clean up the past, and they've given us reason to trust our future; Step Ten helps us focus on what we can do today. With this Step, we can examine how the actions of the day did, or did not, contribute to our growth in sobriety and stability. Keeping us mindful of things that have troubled us in the past, it shows us how we're doing in the present and keeps us on the right track to move ahead into a healthy future. Neither wallowing in what happened nor fantasizing about what hasn't happened yet, we focus instead on what we need to do right now.

We've identified our most glaring character defects in our earlier Step work and have asked to have them removed; however, they generally don't disappear overnight, and our old habits, beliefs, and patterns won't be rooted out without effort over time. That effort takes place as we make changes—thought by thought, action by action, day by day. If we don't make the effort, we slide back into unmanageability and insanity pretty fast. An inventory is necessary so we can both clean up our act and mark our progress as we go.

There are three types of ongoing inventories that are generally suggested. The first of these is the "spot check." This is the practice of staying mindful of our thoughts, behaviors, and motives as the day goes by. It helps us monitor the day's ups and downs, handle new situations and challenges as they arise, and identify familiar patterns when they trip us up. The *Twelve Steps and Twelve Traditions* points out that this helps us in "quieting stormy emotions," especially for those of us who deal with mental illness; our moods and reactions may have something to do with our disorders, and staying mindful of them when they happen enables us to identify both character defects and symptoms as they come into play.

A spot check helps us maintain a steady attitude of honesty and humility. It also keeps us from straying too far down any unhealthy path, whether the cause is character defect or symptom. If I'm checking in with myself three times a day, it's unlikely a whole day will pass without my noticing a symptom getting worse; it's also unlikely I'll let a day go by while I stew over some bit of resentment or do someone harm without realizing it.

The spot check helps me avoid guilt—not because I never make mistakes, but because they come to my attention and I try to promptly admit them. This was an old stumbling block for me: thinking that if I'd made a mistake, there was no correcting it, because I was unwilling to admit I was wrong. My pride caused me to build up walls that caused further damage and deepened my guilt, blocking spiritual growth and ruining peace of mind. By working Step Ten, taking inventory and admitting my wrongs, I can avoid this trap. The humility required by this Step keeps me in right relation to myself, a Higher Power, and other people.

And the spot check helps me maintain my sanity, hour by hour. A sane day is not a "perfect" day—there will be symptoms, mistakes, and character defects cropping up out of nowhere in any given twenty-four-hour period. But sanity can be maintained through mindfulness and a thorough awareness of how I'm doing, in my mind and in the world.

The second type of inventory recommended is the basic daily inventory. Many people do this at the end of the day. Some people do it formally, reviewing their day and writing it down on a piece of paper; others do it more informally, lying in bed before they go to sleep. For the purposes of someone with mental illness, a formal inventory may be more helpful. This allows us to track moods, thoughts, and treatments daily, so that we can keep a record of how our mental health is doing at all times.

The daily inventory also helps us keep track of the quality of our sobriety on a given day. Assessing our thoughts, actions, and interactions with others over the course of the day just past, we try to identify areas of success and areas for improvement. It's important to judge lightly and as impartially as possible; there is no need for self-flagellation when mistakes have been made. Simply identify them, plan to make amends as soon as possible wherever necessary, and determine ways you can do better next time.

During a daily inventory, as opposed to a spot check, we have the space and time to examine our emotions and motives more carefully. We can look a little deeper into the cause of our troubles, the source of emotional distress, and our own role in misunderstandings or conflict. What may have felt like anger in the light of day may turn out, when we have a little distance on it, to have been sadness, guilt, or other more subtle reactions. Harsh words that may have felt justified in the daytime may turn out in an evening's examination to be nothing more than self-righteousness or unnecessary lashing out. Having this distance allows us to see where our character defects caught us by surprise and caused us to act in ways that we regret. We are therefore able to make a clear-eyed assessment of wrongs done, large and small, and prepare to make amends.

In taking daily inventory, it's important to keep a check on rationalization. Explaining away poor choices, whether having to do with our interactions, our daily responsibilities, or our mental health care, will get us nowhere. If I have done nothing to maintain my mental health over the course of the day and instead have skipped meds, canceled appointments, or failed to do any of the things that support my recovery, my inventory is not where I get to justify these poor choices to myself. I have to use the inventory as a place where I am honestly taking stock, or it won't help me.

It's also important in the daily inventory to include things we've done well. Acknowledging my daily successes in my journey toward recovery helps me recognize my strengths as they develop, and gain faith in my own ability to live a healthy, productive, and useful life. The inventory is not intended to cut us down but to keep us accountable to ourselves and the people around us. Taking stock of things well done reminds us that we are making progress in our efforts. While a humble attitude is necessary for the inventory, humility is about *honest* self-assessment, and that includes honesty about our strengths; we should not overlook all that is good in ourselves and our lives.

Many recovering people also find it helpful to take periodic, longer-term inventories, once every few months or every year. This allows us to see how we are changing over time. A periodic inventory shows us evidence of spiritual growth, as we see our relationships improving and our old negative habits falling away. We are able to identify character defects that have left us, and others that linger; we may see things in ourselves that we weren't ready to see when we did our Fourth Step inventory, and this more regular inventory gives us the opportunity to start working on those newly identified issues as well.

We can see patterns emerging over the course of the months and can think about ways to address negative patterns and encourage positive ones. A longer-term inventory allows us to see patterns in our mental health as well and helps us track our progress in managing it. This will help us learn the cycles of our mental illness, so that we can be prepared for it when it flares up.

An inventory—whether taken in a moment of free time during the day, or at day's end, or every few months or a year—is the most practical action we can take to maintain our sobriety and our mental health. By remaining accountable to ourselves, we can be accountable to others. We can finally trust ourselves to do the right thing— not expecting that we'll never make mistakes, but knowing we will take responsibility for them when we do. And we can finally trust that we will take care of our mental health. For much of our lives, we have been unable to rely on ourselves, just as much as others have been unable to rely on us. Now we know that we are capable of managing our mental, emotional, and spiritual health. We know that we are capable of growth and stability. The inventory gives us an opportunity to stay on top of problems, identify areas where growth is necessary, and celebrate progress we have made.

This "maintenance Step" keeps us walking the road of recovery. We see, day by day, our ever-increasing ability to maintain sanity and stability. We see the Promises coming true for us. One of those promises is this: "We will comprehend the word serenity and we will know peace." Turning now to Step Eleven, we begin moving toward a clearer understanding of what peace and serenity mean to us and how we can bring them into our daily lives.

Power

Sought through prayer and meditation to improve our conscious contact with God as we understood Him, praying only for knowledge of His will for us and the power to carry that out.

FOLLOWING THE "MAINTENANCE" WORK OF STEP TEN, in Step Eleven we come to something far more amorphous but equally important. One might say that in this step, we reach for "sustenance." This sustenance is the nourishing ingredient of the whole of our recovery and feeds our ongoing spiritual growth. We have already seen that sobriety is really a "daily reprieve based on the maintenance of our spiritual condition." This Step is where we address our spiritual condition most directly, day after day.

We work this Step regardless of our beliefs—or lack of beliefs— about God, a Higher Power, or any kind of force outside ourselves, because in this Step all we need to do is to regularly access our spiritual core. For some of us, that access comes via God; for others, a sense of a more general Higher Power comes into play; for others, the spiritual source we understand is actually a power within ourselves. It doesn't matter: this is truly the spiritual source *of our own understanding.* But developing that understanding and opening up a channel of communication with it are necessary as we move forward in our recovery.

As many of us know, the ravages of mental illness can destroy a sense of ourselves as spiritual beings. As we recover our mental health, Step Eleven will help us restore that awareness of our own spiritual natures. Prayer and meditation can end the sense of spiritual deadness that many of us have felt. Whether or not we believe in a God, as we work this Step, we find ourselves developing a spiritual life.

"Those of us who have come to make regular use of prayer," it says in the *Twelve Steps and Twelve Traditions*, "would no more do without it than we would refuse air, food, or sunshine. And for the same reason. When we refuse air, light, or food, the body suffers. And when we turn away from meditation and prayer, we likewise deprive our minds, our emotions, and our intuitions of vitally needed support. As the body can fail its purpose for lack of nourishment, so can the soul."

When I first came into the program, this Step bewildered me. I believed in no God, no Higher Power; the idea of prayer was totally foreign because I didn't know who I was praying *to*. But my sponsor insisted that I didn't actually *need* to know that. Sensing that there was a spiritual force at work in the world and in my life, whatever name I chose to give it—even if I identified it as the force of a moral center within myself and others—that was enough. Prayer, then, didn't have to be religious in nature; it could be simply a means of acknowledging that force in some way.

I had heard the AA adage "prayer is asking for guidance, and meditation is listening for the answer." And I knew from working the Steps that if I listened, if I opened my mind and became willing to hear, answers to my deepest and most impossible questions truly did come—whether they came from other sober people, from my moral sense, or from some small, unnamed voice within, which I might have called my spiritual self. It was in meditation that guidance arrived.

And so I began a practice of *my* kind of prayer and meditation. It wasn't too complicated; I simply woke up early, before the house was up and about, and sat in a dark room. I sat and listened. As the chatter of my own day-to-day thoughts faded away, I began to think about some of the larger questions and concerns I was facing. I didn't try to answer them myself. As I had when I turned over my will and my life in Step Three, I simply turned over those questions. To whom? It didn't matter. I'm not a philosopher, and it isn't my job to figure out the nature and source of all things. It is my job to heal my spirit and recover my life. I had been told that I could do that, in part, through prayer and meditation. So I sat in the dark, listening, waiting for guidance from whatever source it wished to come.

I heard a lot of things, unexpected things, both good and bad. But among them was the sound of my own spiritual brokenness and hunger. This startled me, and I didn't want to listen. But I did. Sanity and serenity depended on it. Sitting at my table looking out at the sunrise every day, reading the meditations that clicked for me, I listened to what seemed to be a long-abandoned spiritual self.

I heard anger, shame, regret—things that had divorced me from my own spiritual center to the point where I was no longer certain it was there. I heard disillusionment, denial, and resentment—things that had buried any faith I might have had in a spiritual source. I began to question the wisdom of meditating; at first, it dredged up no small measure of sadness and a great deal of fear that spirituality would be, for me, a thing out of reach.

But the people whose wisdom I sought during this early, tentative period of spiritual exploration said that these things—anger, sadness, doubt, fear—were entirely normal. They told me that spirituality was not always sunshine and roses; on the contrary, sometimes spirituality was bearing witness to sorrow, living through "the dark night of the soul," and that the process of gaining spiritual strength and under-standing was the sometimes painful process of spiritual growth.

I knew very well that a great deal of my alienation from my own spirit and from any spiritual life was related to the fact that mental illness and addiction had beaten me down. I felt abandoned by any kind of spiritual source. I felt anger at the ravages of mental illness and addiction in the lives of people I knew. I felt a total confusion and horror in the face of suicides, self-harm, and the excruciating pain that mental illness sometimes brought. I found no peace with any God and blamed whatever Higher Power there might be for all the devastation I had seen.

There is a great temptation with mental illness to believe fervently or deny absolutely. People with brain disorders know all too well the desperate prayers for comfort or relief when our illness has us in its grip. It's deeply natural for us to long for some kind of comfort, to want some guidance through the labyrinth of the mind, to crave a *reason* for the suffering, and to seek assurance of some reward.

Some of us hold tight to faith and are carried by it through dif-ficult times. Some of us, when the relief we seek doesn't come, feel abandoned by God. These people do not find that comfort, that guidance, that reason, or that certainty of reward. I know people who find a healthy nourishment in religion or spirituality, as well as people whose faith flairs in unhealthy ways when they are symptom-atic. And I know people—I was one of them—who at times have lost the belief that there is comfort or guidance to be found in any spiritual path.

One of the most painful things about mental illness is the sense that one is alone. We may feel locked in our minds, unable to reach others, and sometimes unable even to find ourselves. That sense of isolation is deepened by addiction; our use exacerbates our mental illness, exponentially increases our chaos and the insanity of our lives, and makes us feel ever more lost. These things make it very difficult to believe that something so vague as "spirituality" can bring us any peace.

But as we let go of our addiction and begin to manage our mental illness, stillness and quiet begin to enter our lives. This is where we find room for prayer and meditation. And this is where we begin, slowly and not always painlessly, to search for our spiritual natures once again. After feeling for so long that we are locked in our minds and in the chaos of our lives, the search itself brings peace; and as we search, in prayer and meditation, we open the door to the spirit.

The peace and stillness that we find allow us to listen for guidance—from our moral center, our spiritual core, our conception of a Higher Power, from whatever source with which we feel a connection. And that guidance brings us, inevitably, to greater acceptance. We accept our natures, we accept our lives, we accept our mental conditions. Acceptance, which grows in us as we grow, is an act of spiritual strength. Acceptance—freedom from fighting and the confusion that fighting creates—allows us to see clearly how we need to live our lives day by day. Whatever our concept of a spiritual source may be, if we listen, it shows us the next right thing.

Doing the next right thing, for me, includes not only managing my mental illness but also trying to move beyond it. That entails a mindful balance of managing my mental disorder and knowing that there is more to me than that—including a spiritual nature. My mental illness and my addiction kept me trapped for so long that I began to believe I was nothing more than a "sick" person. When I began managing my disorders, I began to see myself as a *whole* person. I began to move beyond my identity as damaged, flawed, and incomplete. I began to feel a connection to the spiritual core of my self.

Seeing myself as a whole and spiritual person allows me to see what gifts I possess that I can offer to others. One of the great blessings of spiritual development is the way it takes us out of our limited, lonely selves. So, when I do the next right thing, I balance responsible self-care with efforts to contribute to the world. This is a spiritual practice that becomes more natural through prayer and meditation.

The suggestions for daily prayer and meditation set out in the Big Book aren't complicated. It says that we might begin our day by spending some time alone. Many people use this time to read meditation books or Twelve Step literature; those who are religious may find it useful to read literature from their religious denomination. We can review our plans for the day and ask our Higher Power "to direct our thinking, especially asking that it be divorced from self-pity, dishonest or self-seeking motives." Many of us, having spent this time in quietude before the day begins, find we feel more peaceful and centered as we move out into the world for the next twenty-four hours. That sense of peace can be identified as our spiritual self in a state of balance and calm.

It's important for each of us to practice this Step in a way that will be healthiest for us. If simply listening and waiting feels too chaotic or gives rise to frightening or persecutory thoughts, or if we have a history of delusion surrounding the issues of God or religion, we may feel more comfortable with a more structured way of approaching prayer and meditation. Reading meditation books, listening to spirituality CDs, or reading other spiritual literature may be a great approach for us.

When we begin our day in a spiritually centered mind-set, it is an entirely different experience than the unmanageable, often painful days we used to have. Our interactions with others, our approach to work and tasks, and our internal equilibrium are all improved. Our ability to manage our mental illness is greatly heightened: when we spend time each morning reviewing our plans for the day, including our plans for mental health maintenance and recovery, we are fully aware of when we step away from the path of health, and fully aware also when we have success. We are better able to remain mindful of symptoms, to follow our treatment plan, to ask for help without hesitation, and to be useful to someone else. When we spend time in meditation and prayer each morning, we practice acceptance, turning over any resistance we might have, and becoming fully willing to care for ourselves.

As the day goes on, we continue to check in with our spiritual side or with a Higher Power. When faced with conflict, uncertainty, or indecision, the Big Book suggests that we "ask . . . for inspiration, an intuitive thought or a decision . . . We are often surprised how the right answers come after we have tried this for a while. What used to be the hunch or the occasional inspiration gradually becomes a working part of the mind."

As we spend more time in recovery and work Step Eleven with seriousness, open-mindedness, and willingness, we do experience the development of spirituality as "a working part of the mind." We grow more used to consulting our spiritual selves, our Higher Power, or both before we make decisions, or when faced with problems. We open ourselves to guidance, and it comes. For some of us, the guidance may be as simple as the reminder to "do the next right thing." But that reminder is enough, many times, to keep us on the path of recovery and spiritual growth. Soon, "doing the next right thing" isn't just about *not* doing the *wrong* thing; as we practice prayer and meditation, we develop our ability to see what more we can do in the world.

At the end of the day, we review where we've been. For myself, it's been useful to practice Steps Ten and Eleven consecutively. I find a place to be alone, then take my daily inventory, addressing mistakes, planning necessary amends, and noting things I've done well. Then I set aside my notebook and try to focus on the spiritual aspects of my day. Did I go out of my way to help others? Did I check in with my spiritual side now and then, or did I get distracted by the rush of daily life? Did I try to carry a conscious sense of my own spirituality with me as I went through the day? I ask myself these questions, and I also review concerns I've got on my mind. Those I turn over, bearing in mind the rest of Step Eleven: "praying only for knowledge of [God's] will for us and the power to carry that out."

The Step includes that directive for a reason. The fact is, while we've worked a lot of Steps by now and made a lot of progress, we are still prone to grabbing our will and our lives back. It's an old habit, and it dies hard, but if we don't keep a check on it, we'll wind up just as confused and unmanageable as we ever were. So, as we develop the habits of prayer and meditation, the Big Book encourages us to "constantly remind ourselves we are no longer running the show."

Well, then, who is? That's what I wanted to know, and in fact I *still* don't know. As certain as I am that this Step is essential to my serenity, sanity, and sobriety, I occasionally feel like I'm beating my head on the wall with the question of just *who* or *what* is out there, and whether that force has even the slightest interest in my prayers. But when I start beating my head on the wall, I have to remind myself of just how little I know, or can know. Whatever the source, I do know that I see a spiritual nature in others, sense it in myself, and see it at work in the world. Whether I connect with the idea of God, a Higher Power, a creative force, or a moral center, I know that all these things are larger than me, and I know that any one of them can be a source of guidance as I make decisions and move through my days.

That's all I need to know; in fact, *not* knowing much more than that keeps me mindful of my own smallness in the grand scheme of things.

It reminds me that I'm only human, and it keeps me humble. This is where the Serenity Prayer is so useful. In this prayer, we do exactly what Step Eleven asks us to do. We connect with our Higher Power, asking only for knowledge of its will for us and the power to carry that out: "God, grant me the serenity to accept the things I cannot change, the courage to change the things I can, and the wisdom to know the difference."

Prayer and meditation are about becoming aware of our spiritual nature and alert to what it knows and what it can learn from other sources of spiritual sustenance and wisdom. Meditation is one way in which we quiet the mind so that we can hear that wisdom.

The Little Red Book points out that addicts "possess a restless spirit that tends toward overactivity. We not only practiced this by un-controlled [using], but we showed evidence of our intemperance in many other ways." We used to try to still this restlessness with our addictive substance or behavior. Now we need to learn to still the mind and body in other ways. Many recovering people find that meditation is the most spiritually rewarding form of stillness they can find.

The *Twelve Steps and Twelve Traditions* notes that meditation is intensely practical. It may be especially practical for those of us with mental illness. It quiets unsettled emotions and therefore can help us stay de-tached from symptoms; when symptoms come up, we can be aware of them without getting caught up in their emotional force, and we can address them quickly. In meditation, we clear our minds to the best of our ability and maintain a kind of mental balance we haven't experienced before.

Meditation is a practice recommended not only by recovering people but by mental health professionals. There is significant scientific evidence that the regular practice of meditation can cause neurological changes that improve mental health and stability.

And on a spiritual front, meditation develops the clarity we need to maintain ongoing peace. In *One Breath at a Time: Buddhism and the Twelve Steps,* Kevin Griffin writes, "Meditation helps me to connect with my own inner wisdom and thus engage more fully with my life."

But what about prayer? For those of us whose idea of a Higher Power is really a sense of a higher self, or a spiritual core, how exactly do we pray? Really, this is a question about how we *communicate.* Prayer is a means of communicating with the spiritual, however we define it, and wherever we see its origins. People of religious background believe that we are in constant communication with God, whether we are aware of it or not; they believe that "bidden or unbidden, God is present," and we have only to open our hearts to open that channel of communication. The same can hold true for those who feel that a Higher Power is actually a spiritual self. If that's the case, then our spiritual self, always within us, is always accessible. For all spiritual seekers, whether they seek God within or without, communication is a matter of removing the barriers that block our spiritual source.

What exactly are those barriers? I know I came to Step Eleven with plenty. Some were related to my anger and disillusionment. Those are common enough barriers; mental illness isn't the only thing that can make a person angry at their idea of God. Others had to do with my unfamiliarity with and doubts about the actual practices of prayer and meditation: Is there any point to praying if I don't know whom or what I'm talking to? What is prayer, anyway? How is it done?

We know our old way of praying, those foxhole prayers so many of us were fond of while we were still in active addiction, doesn't work. It's been pointed out that they are better termed "demands" than prayers. So we need to think of this practice in a different way. Many people of religious background find prayer a very comfortable and familiar act. And many people who identify themselves as spiritual find use for religious prayers. What I found was that prayer doesn't have to be formal, or structured, or specific, or religious, or even directed to someone or something. It has only to be a sincere opening of our hearts and minds, a turning over of our concerns and troubles, and a listening for guidance. I often return to the words of Step Eleven when I lose track of prayer, and am reminded that I'm asking only for direction in how to live and the strength to live in that way.

So if I'm praying "only for knowledge of His will" (however I wish to interpret "His") and "the power to carry that out," I am *not* praying for the disappearance of my mental illness or the ability to drink like normal people. I am not praying for others to act according to my wishes, or for things to go my way with work, or for rewards for my efforts, or for recognition or praise, or for money or a good parking spot, or for my difficulties to dissolve. These may be wishes, but they aren't prayers.

Buddha is said to have told a follower that each of us has eighty-three problems. We will always have eighty-three problems. One problem may disappear, but another will appear to replace it, so that we always have eighty-three. The follower was extremely upset; how was he supposed to find happiness and peace of mind if he had to have eighty-three problems? The Buddha said, "I can help you get rid of your eighty-fourth problem." "What's that?" the follower asked. The Buddha laughed and said, "Wanting to get rid of your problems."

So we have problems. When we pray, we do not pray for problems to be removed; we pray for guidance in handling them and guidance in moving beyond our problems and into a peaceful relationship with our lives and the world.

So, if we are looking to do the will of a Higher Power, how do we know what it is, or how to separate it from our *own*, not always very healthy will? The reason we don't pray for specific outcomes is precisely because they are often no more than rationalized expressions of our own will. Having recently made our way out of an unmanageable life built on "self-will run riot," we can remember that our will often has no idea what it's doing, and when we live according to it, we get ourselves in quite a mess. We need to seek another source of guidance for our actions.

What we need to understand in this area is that we live in the context of the world, of other people. *The Little Red Book* says, "Our understanding of God's will starts . . . with charitable, loving acts of service to others. We cannot live unto ourselves alone . . . As we interest ourselves in this work and carry it on, we are, to the best of our ability, gaining a knowledge of God's will by the practice of faith, honesty, and unselfish service."

Once, my friend Lora said to me, "The only prayer we ever really need to say is 'Thank you.'" A prayer of gratitude may be the most important one a recovering person can offer, however we choose to say it, to whomever or whatever we speak. We have been pulled from a pit of true despair and devastation. We have been restored to a level of sanity we've never had. And that cannot go unremarked. It is healing to us to remember, and acknowledge, the grace we have experienced. Remembering this, we are reminded also of our responsibilities. To paraphrase words from the Bible, we'd do well to keep in mind: "From those to whom much has been given, much will be required."

Much has been given to us. Therefore, we have a responsibility to share that with others. We are at this point in our recovery filled with experience, strength, and hope. As we delve deeper into our spiritual experience and move on to Step Twelve, where we will focus on how we can be of service, there's a prayer that we might consider. The Prayer of St. Francis goes, in part, like this:

> Make me a channel of thy peace; that where there is hatred, I may bring love; that where there is wrong, I may bring the spirit of forgiveness; that where there is discord, I may bring harmony; that where there is error, I may bring truth; that where there is doubt, I may bring faith; that where there is despair, I may bring hope; that where there are shadows, I may bring light; that where there is sadness, I may bring joy. Grant that I may seek rather to comfort than to be comforted; to understand, rather than to be understood; to love, than to be loved. For it is by self-forgetting that one finds.

Then if we have been comforted, we now find ourselves able to bring comfort; if we have been calmed, we can now bring calm. If our burden has been carried, we are strong enough now to carry it for others. Sanity is the gift we have been given and now can give. As we work Step Eleven, we can meditate on how we can bring our gifts to the world when we work Step Twelve.

Service

Having had a spiritual awakening as the result of these steps, we tried to carry this message to alcoholics, and to practice these principles in all our affairs.

"FAITH WITHOUT WORKS IS DEAD." We read this line in the Big Book more than once. At first, it calls for action toward the immediate, critical project of being restored to sanity as we work the Steps. But when we reach the Twelfth Step, we turn our attention outward toward people who are still suffering. It is because we have worked these Steps, and because we have had a spiritual awakening as the result, that we are now uniquely qualified to be of service to other people suffering from mental illness and addiction.

When we talk about Step Twelve, we generally focus on service work—"tried to carry this message to alcoholics"—but really, it's a three-part step. The first part—"having had a spiritual awakening"— and the last part—"to practice these principles in all our affairs"— are no less important in understanding the Step.

Our spiritual awakenings come in an infinite number of varieties and arrive by just as many means. Many of us couldn't say exactly *when* our awakening took place—we rarely have the date and time written down on a piece of paper. It's hard to say when the total change of personality happened, because usually it has happened over time in a way that wasn't immediately apparent to us.

But it has undeniably happened. We can feel it, others can see it. *The Little Red Book* says, "There should be no difficulty in recognizing the essence of a spiritual experience in the contented sobriety we enjoy, in the responsibility we daily assume, in the amends we make, in willingness to admit our mistakes, in our unselfish interest in helping sick alcoholics [or other addicts] and other persons who are less fortunate than ourselves."

That just about nails it. Prior to our spiritual transformation, we could not claim contentment of any kind, could not manage much in the way of responsibility, could not repair our relationships, could not accept or admit when we were wrong. And with specific regard to service work, we often felt we had to hoard what few resources we had left for ourselves. We were spiritually bone-dry. There was nothing left over to give. Now, through our Step work, fellowship, and other work in the program, we find we have more than enough to share with the people around us. That, in itself, is a spiritual awakening.

No two spiritual awakenings can be said to be alike. Some people hit their knees; some people never see a need to do anything of the sort but come to a new spiritual awareness by another route. The route most of us take is clearly stated in Step Twelve itself: "Having had a spiritual awakening *as the result of these steps.*" The transformation that comes about in us is a direct result of the work we've done so far, and that transformation will continue as we work these Steps again and again over time. The change we see in our thoughts, feelings, and behaviors *is* a spiritual transformation, one we could not create on our own, but one that is clearly taking place.

Consider the profound ways in which we have changed. Step One taught us to recognize our own powerlessness; coming to that realization was painful, but we learned as we worked the Step that we could survive pain without the crutch of our addiction. We also learned, as we came into Step Two, that there was hope: however we chose to define it, we came to the understanding that we would be restored to sanity by a power greater than our own limited selves. Newly hopeful, we felt confident enough to learn that great life lesson taught by Step Three: we must let go and turn over our will and our lives. Having done this and now possessed of the capacity for a new level of honesty, we turned a searchlight on our own histories and interior lives in Step Four. In doing this, we discovered that we had the capacity to conquer many of the fears that had haunted us for so long. As we examined these truths about ourselves, we were relieved of the need to hide ourselves away any longer, and the weight of shame began to lift. It lifted further still when we did our Fifth Step, finally speaking aloud the secrets that had poisoned our spirits for years. In Steps Six and Seven, we spent time in serious thought about our spiritual lives and saw how far we had already come; we found we had developed a degree of humility, bravery, and serenity that would allow us to continue our spiritual development further still. In Steps Eight and Nine, we took a hard look at our actions, past and present, and took responsibility for any damage we needed to repair. In doing this, we ended the excruciating isolation we were living in, developed the capacity for empathy, and began to put others before ourselves. We continued this work in Step Ten, developing a daily spiritual practice of honesty, humility, and action. And in Step Eleven, we begin that ongoing spiritual practice that deepens with meditation and prayer as we "improve our conscious contact" with a Higher Power of our understanding. All those changes, all those ways in which we found resources within ourselves that we didn't know were there, can only be described as a spiritual experience, brought about by the Steps.

Early in my sobriety, I couldn't understand how I would ever experience any kind of spiritual transformation, given my lack of belief in a more traditional God-variety Higher Power. I still believed that spirituality was defined by religious faith. But as I continued working through the Steps, I began to understand spirituality as something broader than that. I could feel myself transforming, could see radical changes in both my behavior and my inner life, and gradually came to realize that there was more to me than I had thought. There was a spiritual self, and that spiritual self was being transformed Step by Step.

As I worked my way through, I came to understand my own spiritual experience as the restoration of hope. Prior to getting sober, I was living in absolute despair, if what I was doing could be described as "living" at all. I had no hope for the future, no hope for myself or for anyone else. I had no hope that things could ever change.

But they did. And I did. And the dark night of the soul lifted as hope began to filter into my life. I began to believe—not in a God, but in possibility. I saw proof everywhere of the resilience of the human spirit, the kindness of strangers, the power of community, the potential in each of us for change—the potential for our spirits to transform. Because I saw this all around me, I began to recognize it in myself. Over time, working with the program, the Steps, and other people, I realized that transformation was not a onetime white-light thing for me; it was an ongoing process and would continue all my life.

We don't need to know when it happened—we don't even need to know what power may have caused it. All we need to be aware of is that it has happened, and this has enabled us to move more freely *and more usefully* in the world.

That usefulness begins the day we walk into our first meeting. Even as the newest of newcomers, our presence offers someone else the chance to reach out to us, and that is an act of service to them. Listening in meetings and in our interactions with other sober people is service work; simply being present when others need us is one of the greatest services we can offer in the human community. Our meetings are rife with opportunities to be useful: we can greet people, offer to be group leaders or treasurers, and set up or clean up the room. These are the basic operations of any group, and offering to do them gives us practice in getting involved in something beyond our own concerns.

Unless we put ourselves to work in this way, a theoretical faith in the program won't get us far. Until we take that vital step beyond ourselves, we cannot hope for ongoing, contented sobriety nor expect the blossoming of emotional, mental, and spiritual growth that takes place when we are at the service of those around us. As the Big Book says, faith without works is dead. We must put that faith—and each of the program's principles—into action.

The *Twelve Steps and Twelve Traditions* says that "the joy of living" is the theme of the Twelfth Step and "action is its key word." It's action in service of others that brings joy. When we work this Step, the Big Book says, "Life will take on new meaning. To watch people recover, to see them help others, to watch loneliness vanish, to see a fellowship grow up about you, to have a host of friends—this is an experience you must not miss." And I have to agree. In Step Twelve, we become a part of a vital, living community of people working together toward the common goals of sobriety, sanity, and spiritual growth. We become a part of that community the moment we walk in the door. But we begin to truly feel the warmth of fellowship when we freely share the gifts that we have been given, without expectation of praise or reward.

When I set out on the path of sobriety, the idea that I could be of use to anyone, in any way, was entirely unexpected. I was used to the ways in which my unwillingness to manage my mental illness and arrest my addiction had caused others pain and struggle. I saw myself as little more than a burden to other people. I had trouble re-conceptualizing my role in the world of others; it was an unfamiliar notion that I had anything of substance to offer other people. It took me some time before I could see all the ways in which I was capable of being of service. It began with recognizing that the very nature of my own struggle—dealing with both mental illness and addiction—was the source of my greatest strength, a strength I wanted to share with others who might need it.

Recovering people with mental illness have a unique and critical capacity to help others. Not only can we be of service to any other addict, to our groups and Twelve Step organizations, to people in our communities, and simply to the people in our lives, but we also have the ability to understand and help people like ourselves, addicts who have struggled with mental illness, in a way that many other people cannot. Those of us who have experience in handling both mental illness *and* addiction are of critical importance to each other. We know better than to put forward uninformed opinions about matters of science and brain chemistry; we know better than to play armchair psychiatrist; we know how essential medication is for the majority of us; and we know that managing both mental disorders and addiction is a major challenge.

But we know one more thing, which matters more than anything else: we know that recovery is possible for us. We are growing by leaps and bounds in our own recovery, and because of this, we can share that vital piece of information with another person: *there is hope.*

Much of the Twelfth Step is about bearing witness. Having walked this difficult and rewarding path ourselves and knowing as we do that this path will take us through our whole lives, we can bear witness to another person's struggles and recovery. Our job in fellowship and service is not to tell another person how it's done, nor is it to carry someone along the path; our job is to walk with them, telling them how *we* did it and how we do it daily, when they ask.

Those of us with mental illness can bear witness to one another in very particular ways. The fact of the matter is, my sponsor has no idea what psychosis is like. She does not know what mania feels like and has never been in the hell of depression. I do, and I have. And because I have been to these places, I can listen more closely and with deeper understanding when other people tell me about similar places they've been, things they've felt, things they've thought, when they were suffering from their mental disorder and when they were not.

The recovering people in my life who deal with mental illness are a crucial resource for me, and I hope I'm a resource for them. They know the landscape of mental illness intimately; they also know the landscape of health. Those of us who are recovering from mental illness and addiction are able to hear one another's stories without judgment and fear. For many of us, recovery may be the first time we have felt so fully understood. It may take some time for us to find the groups and the people who will get it. But we're there, and the more vocal we are, the more supportive we can be.

We can be open with each other in a way perhaps not possible for us with just any recovering person. Openness and honesty are critical to sobriety; all of us need someone with whom we can share our stories completely. As we embark upon the Twelfth Step, we can make it our goal to be that person for someone else. It's said time and again that when we work the Twelfth Step and offer our help to others, they may actually be helping us more than we're helping them. That's not a bad thing as long as we are genuinely trying to be of service; it's just how it works. "Give and you shall receive" is an old and apt saying here. And it's true.

Our service work can expand beyond that, even early in sobriety. We don't have to look far for opportunities. We can join our groups in taking meetings to treatment centers, shelters, prisons, detox centers, or homebound people. We can make calls to newcomers or to just about anyone, and make a connection that will be useful to both ourselves and them. We can offer to tell our story or speak on the Step or topic in our meetings, or get on the list of volunteer speakers in our Twelve Step organization and visit other groups. Simply putting our time and energy to use in service of other recovering people's needs, large or small, is how we carry the message.

We may also be able to offer particular insight not just to other recovering people with mental illness but also to their families or friends when those people have questions about the program and about recovery from mental disorders and addiction as a whole. Families and friends are often in the dark about how their loved one is working toward health, and our experience with that process can help them understand what's going on, what they can hope for, and how they can help. We can also offer to be a contact person for people we meet who deal with dual diagnoses; simply having a phone number for a person who will understand is immeasurably valuable to people who are setting off down this road.

The form of service work people generally talk about the most is sponsorship. Not everyone sponsors or needs to sponsor; it may be that your skills in service work lie elsewhere, or that something about your situation or mental health condition prevents you from sponsoring. All of that is perfectly acceptable, and there are countless other ways to help others and benefit from helping. But those of us who do want to and are able to sponsor reap enormous rewards from the practice.

The central tenant of sponsorship is *attraction, not promotion*. We are not proselytizing. If we *do* proselytize, we will alienate more people from the program and recovery than we help. And it's important to be aware that newcomers may not have quite the same whole-hearted trust of the program that we have developed. People are often skittish—I certainly was—and it's important to let each of us find our own way. Sponsorship is not an opportunity to stand on a soapbox and preach. It is a process of spiritual development, like all service work is. In this case, though, it is a process that two people go through together, developing their own spiritual lives along the way.

One of the most important aspects of being a good sponsor is knowing that you *don't* know everything. You don't have the rulebook, because there isn't one. You have your experience. That's what you can share.

A helpful sponsor is one who has worked and is working the Steps, who feels that he or she has had a personality change as the result of spiritual awakening, and who is active in the program. If we want to meet those prerequisites, we need to work with a sponsor ourselves; our goal is not only to teach but to be taught. We need to go to meetings. And we need to work the Steps. We find a firm foundation in the program, not in our own opinions. As a sponsor, I am useful to my sponsees only insofar as I am actively seeking my own spiritual growth and personal development.

Sponsorship, at its basis, helps us stay sober by helping another person stay sober. For those of us with mental disorders, it also makes us accountable for management of our mental health. If we are sponsoring another person with a mental illness, we are kept mindful of our own responsibility to maintain mental wellness in addition to helping that other person reach mental wellness.

As sponsors, we do not have the option of slipping in our self-care, and as sponsors to people just like ourselves, we are able to help them also stay on top of their mental health management. We are able to dispel myths about mental illness that they may have heard in and out of the program. We can offer encouragement when they are discouraged by the circuitous nature of progress in recovery. We can help them discern when their behaviors, feelings, and thoughts are symptoms of mental illness, and when they are symptoms of addiction.

There are areas a sponsor often advises upon that are specifically affected by mental illness, and we are particularly well suited to helping each other in these areas. Mental disorders impact our relationships, our families, our work lives, our finances, our living situations, and more. In recovery, we may be useful to other people with mental disorders by sharing our experience in managing each of these aspects, working through challenges within them and balancing them with each other. We can talk openly about how mental illness affects us, without fear of judgment and with certainty that the person we're talking to knows what it's like.

In offering insight in personal matters, however, it's essential that both sponsor and sponsee bear in mind that *all you can do is share your experience, strength, and hope.* Your sponsor is not your therapist, psychiatrist, priest, parent, or partner, and you are none of these things to him or her. Your sponsor cannot tell you how to live or what to do. There are plenty of questions you'll have that he or she can't answer and that you, when you are a sponsor, won't be able to answer for someone else either. It's important to recognize both the benefits and the healthy limits of what a sponsor is and what sponsorship is all about.

Sponsorship kills complacency. When we are bearing witness to other people's struggles and successes in their search for sanity and serenity, we are less likely to stagnate in our recovery, because we are walking with them through theirs. This journey carries us along as well. This is one of the reasons that sponsorship is such a vital part of Twelve Step life for both the sponsor and the sponsee. Mutual assistance and support help both parties grow.

Service work teaches me, as both sponsor and sponsee, to live in relationship with others, something I just didn't understand before I worked the Steps. I had relationships, sure, but until I started working with a sponsor, I never fully grasped some essential components of living in the world: responsibility, honesty, and simply giving more than I took were all things that had escaped me for a long time. When I began to work with a sponsor, I began to learn about those things and a whole lot more. And when I began to work with sponsees, my understanding of how to give of myself deepened even further.

Sponsorship offers both challenges and rewards. For one thing, it can take some time to find the sponsor that's right for you. There are as many sponsoring relationships as there are people in the world—no two are alike. I went through three sponsors before I came to the one who's been my sponsor now for some years. Those first sponsors were perfectly good people, and they helped me immeasurably in the difficult early stages of sobriety. Each left me with nuggets of wisdom I'll never forget. But the fit wasn't quite right, and eventually I met someone whom I admired immensely, who made me laugh, whose serenity I found inspiring, and whose take on the world made a great deal of sense to me. I knew she had a lot to teach, and I wanted to learn.

She wouldn't be exactly the right sponsor for everyone, but she's just right for me. Some people would find her not gentle enough; for me, her frankness and honesty are an enormous support. Some people might want more or less contact; for us, coffee weekly and phone calls as needed are perfect. And some people might be taken aback by her willingness to acknowledge the challenges of sobriety and the fact that we are never cured. Once, I was driving cross-country late at night, and I had a sudden craving so powerful I nearly swerved off at the next exit and into town to find a bar. I picked up my phone and called her immediately.

"Where are you?" she asked.

"Just outside Green Bay, Wisconsin," I said, frantic.

"OK," she said. "Keep driving till the craving's gone. If you get to California, call me and I'll come get you." And she hung up.

Now, some people might get nothing out of that. But it made me laugh so hard I totally forgot that I was having a craving at all. And it kept me sober when I needed help.

Sponsoring others has its challenges and rewards as well. The biggest challenge may be maintaining a constant awareness that you cannot save other people—you can't get them sober any faster than they're ready to go, can't keep them from slipping up, can't solve the other problems in their life for them, and shouldn't try. It's essential to maintain an awareness that you are only there as a support, not as a savior. It is the sponsees' job to use you as a resource, not your job to force your help on them. Everyone comes to sobriety in his own way and on his own time—and some people won't come to it at all. Harsh as it may sound, that's not your problem. Your job is to offer your experience, strength, and hope. As long as you're doing that, you're doing your best.

One of my sponsees had a very rough go of early sobriety. She wanted it badly but just couldn't seem to put together more than a few days at a time. We'd meet for coffee, and she'd seem to have decided to stay sober for good—and then she'd show up at the meeting smelling like booze. God knows I understood her struggle and her slips. I'd done the very same thing. At the same time, part of me wanted to swoop in, tell her exactly how to do it (as if I know how anyone other than myself can do it), fix up all her other problems, and Get Her Sober. Instead, I took her car keys when she showed up drunk, and dropped them off at her house the next morning so she could get to work. There were a lot of intoxicated phone calls; there were a lot of tears; and while it was breaking my heart to see her in so much pain, I knew that all I could do, all I *needed* to do, was offer my concern and support.

A year later, she's got one of the most powerful, contented programs I've ever seen. She did what few of us are willing to do: as it says in the Big Book, she went "to any lengths necessary" to get sober. She went to treatment and then to a halfway house; she made her way through her family's abandonment of her and didn't drink over it; she went to meeting after meeting, made sober friends, did service work in several groups, and more. In short, she got *herself* sober, with the help of other people and her Higher Power, and without any interference from me. I admire her immensely, feel lucky to be able to work with her, and learn about sobriety from her every time we meet.

Doing any form of service work helps us do something that's essential for our simple happiness in daily life: getting out of ourselves. *The Little Red Book* is talking about sponsorship here, but it's true of any way we can find to be useful in the program: "[The] cardinal virtue . . . is the momentary loss of self-centeredness." This may be the strongest sign of personality change and spiritual development. As it says in the Promises, "That feeling of uselessness and self-pity will disappear. We will lose interest in selfish things and gain interest in our fellows." And that interest in the people around us allows us to witness the miracles that occur in their lives, and feel gratitude for those that occur in our own.

The miracles I've witnessed in the lives of people I've sponsored have changed my life as well. I've sponsored people who do have mental illness and those who do not. I have seen people go from daily drunks who can hardly function to highly effective, sober, sane people who help others stay clean every day. I've seen people learn to manage even the most severe mental illness, developing goals for themselves about what "sanity" can mean in their lives and working toward those goals step by dedicated step. I've seen people get their lives back, and I've seen people who never felt they had lives worth living develop a passion for life they could never have imagined before. And it's through service work—everything from being a sponsee to being a sponsor, from setting up chairs at the meeting to taking a meeting to a mental health treatment center, from volunteering in the community to living the principles at home—that I've gotten to see these amazing changes occur.

And that's where we come to the third part of Step Twelve: "practice these principles in all our affairs." We can go through the Steps and easily see what those principles are. They include willingness, honesty, acceptance, forgiveness, service, and responsibility. But perhaps above all, as we reach the Twelfth Step and realize that we aren't done—that the Steps continue, paving a path that we can walk our whole lives—the principle of gratitude can light the way.

In our lives, in our relationships, in our work, and in our participation in the larger world, gratitude may be the key. When we open our eyes to all we have been given, there is no way to avoid sheer wonder. We nearly lost our lives to our addiction and our unmanaged mental illness, and we are getting those lives back, more and more each day. The fact that we have not only survived but are now beginning to thrive is a miracle in itself. So many of us were barely alive before, and the lives we had were shot through with pain. Now, we are feeling the fullness of life and have more than enough to spare for people who need our inspiration, our help, and our hope. That we have made it and come so far are something for which we must have indescribable gratitude.

Every person I've ever met with long-term, serene sobriety speaks of how the Steps reveal new aspects of themselves with every working. Getting through the Steps just once won't show us all the promise and discovery that they hold. Our greatest opportunity—to heal, to grow, and to serve—lies in putting the principles into practice in our daily lives. When we do this, we find new reasons to be grateful for every aspect of our existence, from our relationships to our livelihood to the simple tasks our lives require. This gratitude becomes a habit, a way of seeing the world, and it is spiritual nourishment that all of us need.

Our mental disorders have not gone away, and they won't. We are still addicts. Healing, for us, is not about erasing simple physiological fact. Healing is an ongoing process of spiritual discovery and growth, available to anyone willing to do the work. Recovery makes no promises about what will happen to us as we move through life; we will still hit crises, feel pain, struggle with our illnesses, and experience loss. But recovery does give us the strength and peace of mind to meet these things with sanity and grace.

Living with mental illness and addiction is a challenge, no question about it. But the Twelve Step program gives us a host of tools to help us meet that challenge. By taking full responsibility for our lives—actively managing our mental disorders, actively working an addiction recovery program, and continuing to develop our spiritual health—we do find that sanity, sobriety, and stability are possible for us.

There was a time we could not have imagined these things for our-selves, a time when we had no hope. And there will be times that our mental disorders may tell us to give up hope again. But we are fully capable of hanging on to it now. We have evidence that the program works, in our own lives and in the lives of people around us. We have every practical reason for the miracle of hope.

What It's Like Now

WHAT IS IT LIKE TO COME ALIVE? What is it like to be transformed? Hard to put into words. These are things you will feel for yourself and in fact are probably feeling already. I know that had someone told me I would feel transformed, would undergo a complete personality change, would see that the Promises do come true, would understand that hope can be mine, I would have thought they were either lying or deluded. I would have dismissed all this as Pollyanna nonsense and returned to the small room of my own despair, where things were bleak and familiar, reliable in their hellishness, where I lived in the known quantity of misery that I called my life.

So perhaps it's hard to believe someone when they tell you about "what it's like now." But "now" is an extraordinary place. It is a place of possibility, a door opening outward into the world. And the world is no longer the terrifying place I once thought it was; now it, too, is all about possibility, about things to be learned and lived and loved. The world is where I move beyond my limits, beyond my own self-doubt, beyond myself, and into a vital engagement with others and with life. And the Steps are what show me the way back into the world.

One of the Promises I like best is this one: "We will comprehend the word serenity and we will know peace." It's true. A friend of mine joked once that just because we *comprehend* the word serenity doesn't mean we always *have* it. This is also true. Serenity is not a constant companion, but it's there for me more often than not, and I do know peace. This is a miracle in itself. That I have any comprehension whatsoever of peace, after a lifetime of chaos and destruction, shocks me; and yet peace is there, day after day, filtering through even the darkest days.

And there are dark days. Just as I know peace, I also know frustration, difficulty, loss, and all the rest of the challenges life brings. I know illness; my mental disorder has not been magically removed by sobriety, and it won't be. But I also know recovery—which would not have been possible for me if I'd never gotten clean. The difference between now and the years when I lived in chaos is that I now have the knowledge, the tools, and the support to handle any kind of challenge, any kind of change. These things will not be easy and have not been. But now they are simply part of the fabric of experience, things to be met with acceptance, responsibility, and willingness, rather than crises to be run from out of fear.

You've heard that the Twelve Steps are "a program for living." And they are. They act as a map for navigating the sometimes tumultuous waters of life. They help us through the difficult passages, and they teach us to take joy in the discoveries we make as we go. What I am discovering as I work and rework the Steps over time is that there is no end to this journey. If I want to reap real knowledge and real understanding from the Steps, if I want to see real growth and change by working them, if I want to have a spiritual experience as their result, I need to work them again and again. I need to put them into practice in my daily life. The Steps are not chapters in a book. The Steps truly *are* a way of learning to live. The point, for me, is not to complete a tidy Twelve Step checklist. The point is to come back to life, to keep living, to transform.

And what is that like? That's for you to discover. I can only speak to my own experience and bear witness to the miracles in others' lives. Recovery from addiction is an ineffable process, and mental wellness is hard to describe as well. Recovery and mental health look different for every one of us. But we can reach a place we had not dreamed of—if we make the effort, if we give ourselves over to the process, if we go to any lengths necessary to find our way to solid ground. We can find an ever-evolving "now" that is full of possibility and hope.

It will not always be easy. There will be no magic cures. But there will be things that are more solid, more durable, and more lasting than the fantasy of perfection we once had. Things like honesty, acceptance, and joy. And believe me when I say that there will be joy.

Appendix A

THE TWELVE STEPS OF ALCOHOLICS ANONYMOUS*

1. We admitted we were powerless over alcohol—that our lives had become unmanageable.

2. Came to believe that a Power greater than ourselves could restore us to sanity.

3. Made a decision to turn our will and our lives over to the care of God *as we understood Him.*

4. Made a searching and fearless moral inventory of ourselves.

5. Admitted to God, to ourselves, and to another human being the exact nature of our wrongs.

6. Were entirely ready to have God remove all these defects of character.

7. Humbly asked Him to remove our shortcomings.

8. Made a list of all persons we had harmed, and became willing to make amends to them all.

9. Made direct amends to such people wherever possible, except when to do so would injure them or others.

10. Continued to take personal inventory and when we were wrong promptly admitted it.

11. Sought through prayer and meditation to improve our conscious contact with God *as we understood Him*, praying only for knowledge of His will for us and the power to carry that out.

12. Having had a spiritual awakening as the result of these steps, we tried to carry this message to alcoholics, and to practice these principles in all our affairs.

* The Twelve Steps of AA are taken from *Alcoholics Anonymous*, 4th ed., published by AA World Services, Inc., New York, NY, 59–60.

Appendix B

Described here in their own words, these support groups hold regular meetings in many locations. For meetings in your area, check online or in your local telephone book.

Alcoholics Anonymous: www.aa.org
212-870-3400
Mailing address:
    A.A. World Services, Inc.
    P.O. Box 459
    New York, NY 10163
Location:
    A.A. World Services, Inc., 11th floor
    475 Riverside Drive at West 120th Street
    New York, NY 10115

Alcoholics Anonymous is a fellowship of men and women who share their experience, strength, and hope with each other that they may solve their common problem and help others to recover from alcoholism.

Double Trouble in Recovery: www.doubletroubleinrecovery.org
718-373-2684
    P.O. Box 245055
    Brooklyn, NY 11224

Like AA, DTR is a fellowship of men and women who share their experience, strength, and hope with each other. For those in DTR, the goal is to solve their common problems and help others to recover from their particular addiction(s) and manage their mental disorders(s). For more information on DTR, please also visit www.hazelden.org/dtr.

Dual Diagnosis Anonymous: www.ddaoforegon.com
877-222-1332
Mailing address:
> P.O. Box 2883
> Portland, OR 97208
Location:
> 521 SW 11th Avenue, 2nd floor
> Portland, OR 97205

DDA is a peer support group based on an authorized version of the Twelve Steps of Alcoholics Anonymous plus an additional five Steps that focus on dual diagnosis (mental illness and substance abuse).

Dual Recovery Anonymous: www.draonline.org
913-991-2703
> DRA World Network Central Office
> P.O. Box 8107
> Prairie Village, KS 66208

DRA is an independent, nonprofessional, Twelve-Step self-help membership organization for people with the dual diagnosis of chemical dependence and emotional or psychiatric illness—both illnesses with physical, psychological, social, and spiritual effects.

Emotions Anonymous: www.emotionsanonymous.org
651-647-9712
> EA International
> P.O. Box 4245
> St. Paul, MN 55104

A Twelve Step program for those seeking emotional health, EA is composed of people who come together in weekly meetings for the purpose of working toward recovery from emotional difficulties.

Narcotics Anonymous: www.na.org
818-773-9999
> P.O. Box 9999
> Van Nuys, CA 91409

The NA Fellowship's vision is that every addict in the world has the chance to experience the NA message in his or her own language and culture and find the opportunity for a new way of life.

About the Author

Marya Hornbacher is an award-winning journalist and the Pulitzer Prize–nominated author of three books. Her best-selling memoirs *Madness: A Bipolar Life* and *Wasted: A Memoir of Anorexia and Bulimia* have become classics in their fields, and her critically acclaimed novel *The Center of Winter* is taught in universities all over the world. Hornbacher's work has been published in sixteen languages. She lectures regularly on writing, addiction recovery, and mental health.

About Hazelden Publishing

As part of the Hazelden Betty Ford Foundation, Hazelden Publishing offers both cutting-edge educational resources and inspirational books. Our print and digital works help guide individuals in treatment and recovery, as well as their loved ones.

Professionals who work to prevent and treat addiction also turn to Hazelden Publishing for evidence-based curricula, digital content solutions, and videos for use in schools, treatment and correctional programs, and community settings. We also offer training for implementation of our curricula.

Through published and digital works, Hazelden Publishing extends the reach of healing and hope to individuals, families, and communities affected by addiction and related issues.

For information about Hazelden publications, please call 800-328-9000 or visit us online at hazelden.org/bookstore.